Education From A Biblical Worldview®

Faculty Training Manual

An introductory course in basic Christian philosophy of education

Authors

E. Daniel Schneider
Daniel J Smithwick

All scripture quotations are taken from the King James Version of the Holy Bible

This manual belongs to-

_____

Additional copies may be ordered from-

Nehemiah Institute, Inc.
3735 Harrodsburg Rd., Suite 150
Lexington, KY 40513
1-800-948-3101
http://nehemiahinstitute.com

June 2004, 1st printing
February 2013, 2nd printing
May 2015, 3rd printing
May 2018, 4th printing

Table of Contents

How to Use This Book

This book was written as a text for a teacher-training course entitled "Education from the Biblical Worldview". However, the book itself can be used in a number of ways.

For individuals:

1. Read for personal growth. Individuals may read this book for gaining information and inspiration on the subject of education and worldview.

2. Take as a course for credit. Individuals may receive credit from the Nehemiah Institute in the form of a certificate of completion. For details contact:

Nehemiah Institute
3735 Harrodsburg Rd, #150
Lexington, KY 40513
1-800-948-3101
office@nehemiahinstitute.com

As a group:

1. Individuals may wish to meet together on a regular basis and use the study questions as a basis for discussion. A Leader's Guide may be obtained from Nehemiah Institute.

2. Members of informal groups may take the course for credit. Contact the above address for details.

3. An entire teaching staff as a group: **We believe the most effective way to utilize this book is for an entire teaching staff to take this course together, meeting regularly and using the study questions. We strongly suggest that the headmaster (principal) of the school lead the discussion sessions using the Leader's Guide.**

4. Teaching staff members for credit: Teachers taking the course as a group can be awarded certificates of completion. Contact the above address for details.

Forward

Dan Smithwick

The past three decades have witnessed a remarkable growth in private Christian education, both in Christian day schools and in homeschooling. The effort has not been in vain. Standardized test scores repeatedly show that students in private Christian education far outpace their counterparts in public schools. It is reported that all homeschool students applying at Harvard last year were accepted. A recent study by Education Policy Analysis Archives of nearly 12,000 homeschool families, stated: "It is readily apparent that the median scores for home school students are well above their public/private school counterparts in every subject and in every grade."

On the other hand, public schools continue to deteriorate- academically, morally and in safety. The number of shootings and killings in public schools, even by little boys, have shaken our nation into disbelief. We keep asking, Why? The answers are as varied as people offering explanations. Several years ago President Clinton announced the standard establishment answer- more teachers, more programs, more money- i.e., more of the same. What should we expect for this? More of the same.

This study is an attempt to answer 'What has gone wrong in public/government schools?' and to provide the answer for what is right about education. Responsibility for education of children was misplaced over a century ago through the efforts of Mann, Dewey, et al. Christ-centered education was replaced with so-called child-centered education. When this transition began in the mid nineteenth century, there still continued a strong Judeo-Christian ethic in the classroom. Prayer and reading of scriptures were also a normal part of the school's activities. When state-run education began, it borrowed the spiritual capital present in schools and because of that; it 'survived' for many decades.

Speaking of early American educators, R.J. Rushdoony said, "Absorbed almost entirely in the process of education, as a rule, it never occurs to these good men that the concepts that they took for granted of a good society were purloined from the Christian heritage that they have studiously ignored or denied." Without faith in God and fear of the Lord as a focus of education, spiritual capital was not being replenished. Now it appears that the spiritual capital has been spent and that the system is coming unglued. The apostle Paul gave us a clear warning, "And He is before all things, and in Him all things hold together." Col. 1:17 Another way of saying this would be, "Things not in Him don't hold together." How long it can continue is uncertain, but some are saying the end of public/government education is near.

Strange Bedfellows

We assert the mixing of school and civil government is not only bad business, but also bad theology. Education of youth is simply not a government function, biblically speaking. Government schools should not be reformed; rather they should be dismantled, though carefully. What is truly needed is a thoughtful plan for separating school and state.

It was precisely the mixing of school and government that was the heart and soul of Dewey's pedagogical reasoning. In 1894 Dewey accepted the position of chairman of the Department of Philosophy, Psychology and Pedagogy at the University of Chicago. It was here that Dewey established his Laboratory School. As noted by education expert Samuel L. Blumenfeld, "Here was, indeed, a master plan, involving the entire progressive educational community, to create a new socialist curriculum for the schools of America, a plan that was indeed carried out and implemented. --- he put forth his collectivist concepts of an organic society, the social individual, the *downgrading of academics* (emphasis mine), and the need to use psychology in education."

In 1897 Dewey published his *My Pedagogic Creed* in which he stated, among other beliefs, "I believe that education, therefore, is a process of living and not a preparation for future living; I believe that education is the regulation of the process of coming to share in the social consciousness; and that adjustment of individual activity on the basis of this social consciousness is the only sure method of social reconstruction… I believe that every teacher is a social servant set apart for the maintenance of proper social order and the securing of the right social growth. I believe that in this way the teacher always is the prophet of the true God and the usherer in of the true kingdom of God."

Dewey got his wish- a messianic school system, but without the God of the Bible. What his messianic system has gotten us is a mess. As Blumenfeld stated, "More than ninety years have gone by since Dewey set American education on its progressive course. The result is an education system in shambles, a rising national tide of illiteracy and the social misery caused in its wake." "Bread alone" didn't work.

Dan Schneider has given us a masterpiece in philosophy of education. Dan has served the cause of biblical education for over forty years as a teacher, school administrator, school board member, researcher, and consultant. He has a B.A. degree in history and an M.A. degree in education. His post graduate studies include studies in Christian School Administration at Oral Roberts University, an internship in Principle Approach with the Foundation for American Christian Education (F.A.C.E.), and Biblical Worldview Studies at Summit Ministries. Dan has also been a close friend over these 40 years and I can personally testify not only to his academic expertise in philosophy of education but in his application of principles from generational testimony of Christian faithfulness of Dan and his wife's children and grandchildren. Currently Dan is serving as family life pastor in a church in Minnesota.

Introduction

The terms "worldview" and "biblical worldview" are relatively new to the common vocabulary of Christian educators. Thirty years ago, these terms were rarely used. Then in the early 1990's through a variety of events and circumstances, "worldview" became popular with Christian educators.

One of the events that led to an increased interest in "worldview" was the publicity given to Summit Ministries of Colorado by popular Christian radio personality, Dr. James Dobson. The mission of Summit Ministries is to provide worldview training for high school seniors at summer camps. Dr. Dobson's teenage son had such a meaningful experience at Summit's camp that his father gave high praise and recommendation for Summit on the "Focus on the Family" radio program which is heard regularly by millions of Christians.

At about this same time Summit Ministries published curriculum for a high school level course on the biblical worldview. Other ministries, such as Wallbuilders, Inc. of Texas, came out with material such as the very popular and effective video, "America's Godly Heritage," which stirred many Christians to a new appreciation of the blessings of the biblical worldview on America's history. Other ministries, often of the grassroots or homespun variety (as opposed to larger, established ministries) came out with new books, tapes, and videos that talked about the biblical worldview.

By the late 1990's "worldview" had become a buzzword. Parents wanted education with a biblical worldview, and almost every Christian school in the country promised education with a biblical worldview. School boards and administrators made great effort to include terms like "Christian worldview" or "biblical worldview" on their websites and all their brochures and promotional materials.

The question arises, "Is this new focus on worldview in Christian education the result of some significant change in the nature of the education process in these schools, or is it just placing fresh emphasis on something that has always been an integral part the education provided by these schools?" In other words, has a sound biblical worldview been the result of a Christian school education all along, or have Christian schools made recent adjustments to their education programs that result in a stronger biblical worldview in their graduates?

Many Christian educators believe they have been providing education with a biblical worldview all along. Others adjusted like adding the Summit Ministries "Understanding the Times" worldview course to their high school curriculum.

Parents are demanding worldview education. Christian schools are promising it. But how can we tell if a high school graduate does obtain a biblical worldview in his Christian education? Awareness has grown for the need for a tool of objective measurement.

Since 1986 the Nehemiah Institute has been testing high school students on their worldview through its PEERS testing program. The PEERS test evaluates the worldview philosophy held in five areas: Politics, Economics, Education, Religion and Social Issues (PEERS). Approximately 115,000 Christian high school students and faculty have been tested over the last twenty years from over 1,000 Christian schools. Though no test is perfect and can obtain a complete consensus from all Christians on every point included in such a test, the PEERS test is the most comprehensive and objective measure of worldview in existence. What does the data from the PEERS test tell us? Are scores on the rise since "worldview" has become a buzzword, or are they staying about the same?

1

Actually, PEERS test scores of students from most Christian schools have been going down over the last thirty years, as the chart below illustrates.

PEERS Trend Chart

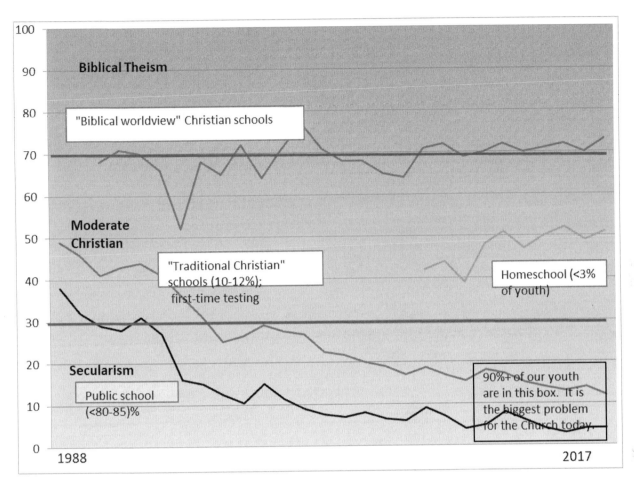

The indication is that despite the renewed interest in worldview education, Christian school education is losing ground in this area. A growing number of leaders in Christian education are realizing the need for more comprehensive measures to strengthen Christian schools in worldview education. Mature biblical worldview education can be achieved, as illustrated in the above chart, but it requires intentional change by the school's leadership.

A major area of concern is teacher education. Teachers with degrees from secular colleges and universities receive no instruction from a biblical worldview. On the contrary, secular education is dominated by an anti-Christian worldview.

Teacher training from a sound biblical worldview is even scarce in Christian colleges. Most Christian college education departments are in the business of preparing Christians to teach in public schools. Most students pursuing teaching degrees in Christian colleges are taught from the same textbooks that are used in secular colleges and universities. In fact, most Christian schoolteachers develop their philosophy of Christian education outside of their formal college training.

Christian educators who want to grow in their understanding of a biblical worldview have very few options. Some worldview ministries offer seminars for pastors and educators, but teachers must be transported to distant locations and the number that can be accommodated is limited. Other ministries, like the Nehemiah Institute, offer seminars that can be presented onsite in individual schools. Both approaches are effective but limited in the number of educators that can be accommodated and in the amount of material that can be covered in a limited time span.

A third option is *Education from the Biblical Worldview (EBW)*. Through this course, Christian educators can grow in their understanding of the biblical worldview at their own pace without the expense of traveling to a seminar or bringing speakers to their schools.

There are several other advantages in taking this course. The amount of material covered in *Education from the Biblical Worldview* is much greater than can be covered in a day-long or even a week-long seminar. A unique feature of this course is that its content is designed to meet the specific concerns of Christians directly involved in education. The course is designed by educators with the purpose of focusing on specific biblical principles that directly affect the education process.

Also, this course provides the blessing of accountability. Specific requirements must be met before certification of completion can be granted. Feedback is given in the form of grades and comments from interaction with fellow teachers and the class leader.

Since the 1960's most state teacher certification requirements include classes in multiculturalism, diversity training, or some other form of politically correct, humanistic indoctrination. The enemies of Christianity have had total and unhindered access to influence American education with their form of worldview education. Until now, there has been very little presented from a Christian worldview to counter this powerful campaign. *Education from the Biblical Worldview* will give Christian educators perspective and insight that will enable them to understand the underlying issues of the worldview conflict in education, and it will arm them with truth to carry on the battle.

How to Use This Course

The entire teaching staff together:

It is easy, even in small schools, for teachers to compartmentalize. Children of different ages have different needs. Teachers tend to focus on the specific concerns of teaching their grade level or subject area. Often the big picture of the overall education of the child is pushed onto the proverbial "back burner" while most of the focus is spent on each individual teacher's concerns for the immediate here and now of her own classroom. We often see this tendency during the days right before school starts in the fall. Teachers tend to prefer using this time to prepare their individual classrooms rather than attend orientation sessions that focus on vision or philosophy. This is typical of the tendency to give attention to the urgent at the expense of the important.

We believe it is extremely important to keep the big picture in the foreground rather than in the background. It is the role of the headmaster to articulate and maintain the vision and to impress upon the entire teaching staff the importance of keeping the vision foremost in their minds. The vision is what gives unity to the ministry. Teachers should be constantly referring to the overall vision of the school as the basis of decision making for the planning of their own classroom activities.

Therefore, we highly recommend that this course be taken as a group, that the entire teaching staff take it together, and that the headmaster of the school lead the sessions. We believe there are several distinct advantages of doing it this way:

1. Unity of vision. The entire staff is covering the same material at the same time. Certain concepts will emerge as important to the vision of the school. Unity in the ministry will be strengthened by a common understanding of these basic concepts which will become reference points for the ongoing work of the ministry.

2. Customized emphasis. The headmaster knows the strengths and weaknesses of his staff, and he will get to know them even better through the interaction of the discussion sessions throughout the course. He can spend more time and emphasis on those areas he knows his staff needs and he can treat more lightly those areas where his staff is already strong.

3. Setting priorities. The very fact that the entire staff is setting aside time to meet regularly to focus on the overall purpose of the ministry makes a statement. If the biblical worldview is important to your Christian school, time and energy must be spent on it. It does not come by osmosis. It is not likely to become a high priority in a school without deliberate attention and effort. Using this course as a staff project will make the biblical worldview a priority in the minds of the teachers, the students, and the parents.

The group sessions:

There are ten lessons in the course. You may want to meet twelve times, including an introductory meeting and a final session if you choose to take the optional final exam. We suggest you schedule them weekly or biweekly, depending on what best fits your school's schedule and depending on how quickly you want to cover the material. Allow at least one hour for each session. The leader's guide provides suggestions for leading the group sessions. Optional questions for discussion, written quiz questions, and a final exam are provided. The leader may choose to give assignments to be completed for each session. For more details consult the leader's guide.

A note about the perspective of this course:

College professors and textbooks in education usually portray themselves as neutral or impartial when presenting conflicting educational theories. In this course we will make the case that it is impossible to be neutral since everyone has a set of presuppositions called a worldview that causes him or her to form opinions on everything. Upon careful reading of most college textbooks, it is possible to uncover an author's presuppositions no matter how hard he tries to present himself as neutral. College professors who claim to be impartial will usually reveal their bias and prejudice over time.

In this course we make no pretenses of neutrality. This course is written from the biblical worldview and for this we offer no apology. We make judgmental statements in every lesson. Ultimately, we are no different from secular authors in that we have a definite perspective to communicate. The big difference is that we make no hypocritical pretenses to impartiality.

Likewise, we make no pretenses of infallibility. Only the Bible is infallible. If any of the views presented in this course conflict with the Bible, we implore you to notify us. It is our desire to be biblically correct. We submit the entire content of this course to the authority of the Word of God.

The Importance of Philosophy

In past generations most textbooks had a short section in the beginning of the book entitled "To the Student." This was a message to the student reader explaining why the material in the textbook was important. It gave a rationale for taking the course.

Along with a "To the Student" section these textbooks also contained a section entitled "To the Teacher." This was a message to the teacher that presented an explanation of the philosophy behind the course.

Both messages dealt with giving reasons why the material in the book was important. The fact that books seldom contain "To the Teacher" and "To the Student" messages is illustrative of one of the major problems that *Education from the Biblical Worldview* addresses. There seems to be very little concern about the underlying philosophy of educational materials today. In fact, there is little concern about educational philosophy in general. Chances are that if modern textbooks did have introductory sections addressed to the student and to the teacher, readers would skip them anyway.

Whether it is stated in writing or not, every piece of educational material ever written is based upon someone's philosophy. Likewise, every teaching method ever used in a classroom is also based upon someone's philosophy of education. Neglecting to state the underlying philosophy or to reflect upon it does not make it go away. It is there behind the scenes controlling, governing, ruling, and dictating every aspect of the educational process. Yet little time and attention is given toward examining underlying philosophy of education.

One of the reasons philosophy is neglected is the assumption that there is basically one common philosophy from which all educational materials and methods are derived. This belief assumes that there is a common consensus or a common knowledge about education that is based upon "common sense." "After all," this assumption would say, "Don't all colleges, whether Christian or secular, teach education classes that are 90% the same?"

Along with this assumption is a common attitude that philosophy of education really doesn't matter. Once a teacher gets into the "real world" of her classroom she must rely on her own wisdom from experience, "common sense," personal wit and wisdom, and teacher instinct. This attitude isolates the study of philosophy from the "real world." Philosophy is seen as a necessary evil that must be studied to get a degree in education (though this requirement is being dropped by an increasing number of colleges). As far as having any practical value, this attitude sees philosophy as of little use.

But what if the current common consensus about education is wrong? What if the common consensus disagrees with the Bible? What if education courses in Christian colleges should be 100% different from secular colleges rather than 90% the same? What if twenty-first century "common sense" is different from nineteenth century "common sense?"

Ideas do have consequences. If an underlying philosophy is based upon truth it will have positive consequences. If it is based upon error, it will have negative consequences. The Bible is the source of truth. Educational philosophy based upon the Bible will have positive consequences. Philosophy based upon unbiblical assumptions will have negative consequences. Therefore, it behooves us as Christian educators to examine our practices to discover their underlying philosophy, and to then compare the assumptions of that philosophy with biblical truth.

This requires humility. It is not easy to examine our assumptions. Some of them may be unbiblical and require change in our practices.

The title of this course is *Education from the Biblical Worldview*. To educate from a biblical worldview, we need to have a biblical worldview ourselves. We are all in the process of forming our own biblical worldview. The Bible calls it renewing our minds. "*And be not conformed to this world: but be ye transformed by the renewing of your mind, that ye may prove what is that good, and acceptable, and perfect, will of God.*" (Romans 12:2). Renewing our minds is a process. Salvation comes the instant we place our trust in Jesus Christ. A renewed mind is not instantaneous. A biblical worldview comes over time. Even the most vocal advocates for biblical worldview education started out with secular worldviews, and none of us can claim we have yet obtained a pure biblical worldview. The key is our attitude. We must remain teachable.

Our goal is to develop our own biblical worldview and to allow it to govern every aspect of our teaching. This includes not only the content of what we teach, but also our teaching methods. Just as I Peter 3:15 exhorts us to "*be ready always to give an answer to every man that asketh you a reason of the hope that is in you,*" Christian educators should be able to give biblical justification for all they do in a classroom. This will require that we examine our assumptions. It will require that we reflect on the underlying philosophy of education that determines our choice of practices.

This is not a time-wasting academic exercise. Contrary to popular opinion, examining philosophy of education is very practical. If our philosophical assumptions are unbiblical, we will be affecting every one of our students negatively. This is why James warns us, "My brethren, be not many masters (teachers), knowing that we shall receive the greater condemnation." (James 3:1). On the other hand, if our teaching practices are based firmly upon a biblical worldview we will experience very real positive results. The fruit of teaching based upon a biblical worldview will bless all those who experience it. Not only will it impart a biblical worldview to the students, it will develop young men and women who are clear thinkers and much stronger academically and intellectually than those educated by a secular philosophy of education. The Church will be strengthened, and the nation will be better for it. As a matter of fact, clear thinking Christians who have a biblical worldview is America's only hope to avoid the consequences of its downward slide toward self-destruction.

Most importantly men and women with renewed minds "prove what is that good, and acceptable, and perfect will of God" (Romans 12:2). They become a light to the world. They are a witness that gives glory to God.

Philosophy: The Original School Glue

Just as we, as evangelicals, have come to realize that a church is not a building, so too we, as educators, must keep in mind that a school is not a building. The word used in the Bible that translates into the English word, "church" is ekklesia, a Greek word that refers to an assembly of people. In the New Testament, "church" meant the body of believers. The use of the word, "church," to refer to the place or the building where Christians meet is not the primary meaning of the word. However, over the years this secondary meaning has eclipsed the primary meaning for many people. We have a similar situation with the use of the word, "school." As the word is most commonly used today, it refers to a building, but the word means much more than a place. Buildings do not define a school.

A school is an organization engaged in the process of providing education. There are a variety of types of schools depending upon the purpose of the school. Every school has objectives or goals. These goals are listed in the school's statement of purpose. In Christian schools we usually refer to these as mission statements.

A school's mission statement is based upon a philosophy or set of beliefs about education. Differences in philosophy are what ultimately determine differences from one school to another.

This brings us to a very important meaning of the word, "school," and one on which we want to place great emphasis. "School" also refers to a set of beliefs, as in "school of thought," or as in the expression, "He belongs to the old school (old way of thinking)." When we use "school" in this sense, we get in touch with the fact that schools are, or should be, defined by their philosophy.

We say "should be" because this is often not the case. Today mission statements often have very little to do with what actually takes place in the classroom. Frequently we are asked to recommend a "good" Christian school or Christian college. This is an increasingly more difficult question to answer. Since mission statements are often ignored in the everyday practices of Christian institutions, they are not reliable statements of how "good" a school is. Furthermore, school principals and academic deans abdicate their responsibility as guardians of the mission statement and allow individual teachers to operate independently of any official school philosophy of education. Many Christian colleges, for example, have some science professors teaching evolution while others teach a creationist perspective.

Below is a summary of PEERS testing at 29 Christian colleges and universities from 1996-2014. This included schools from very large to very small, of Christian higher education. It is evident that even in our 'most prestigious' Christian education institutions, much work remains to be done to ensure that we are equipping young men and women with a mature and consistent biblical worldview.

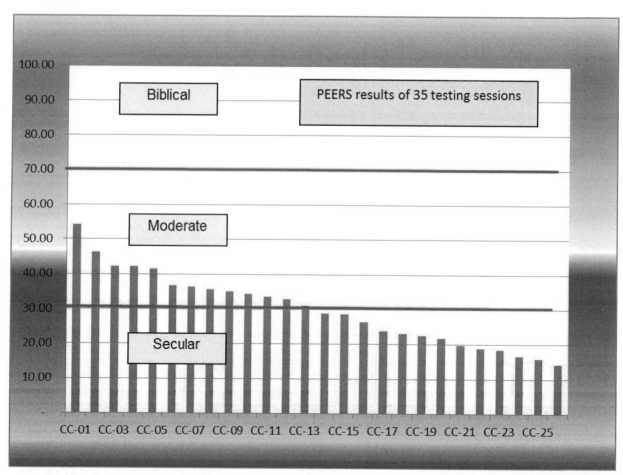

The same is true for Christian elementary and secondary schools. The philosophy of education governing one classroom can be radically different from the next. This is not to say diversity in teacher personality and teaching style is unwelcome. That kind of diversity gives glory to God, but philosophical diversity is something else. Philosophical diversity weakens a school. Unity of philosophy and vision strengthens a school. Philosophical unity is the school's glue.

We believe *Education from the Biblical Worldview* can be an effective tool for strengthening philosophical unity in a school. This is why we recommend that an entire teaching staff take it together. This means both high school and elementary teachers together. Each teacher plays a part in fulfilling a school's mission. It must be kept in mind that it is just that, a part. Every teacher's part should fit into the whole, which is the mission of the school.

Studying the biblical worldview and reflecting on the school's vision as an entire staff will clarify the school's educational philosophy in each individual teacher's mind and strengthen his or her convictions. Knowing that every teacher in a school is of a like mind philosophically will encourage each individual teacher. Secular thinking wars against the biblical worldview. Knowing that every member of a school faculty is in philosophical unity will encourage individual teachers to stand firm on the truth.

Lesson 1

Defining Worldview

Goals:

1. To gain a deeper understanding of what a worldview is.
2. To gain a deeper appreciation of the importance of the biblical worldview.

Assignment:

1. Read Lesson 1.
2. Write answers to Study Questions below.

Study Questions:

1. What is a worldview?
2. What do we mean by "Life on earth is a worldview war?"
3. Explain what "dangerous substitutions" means to a person's worldview. Why are they dangerous?
4. Explain how a wrong worldview will lead to bad education.
5. Explain the definition of education given in this section of the Course Manual.
6. Explain how worldview inconsistency is a problem in Christian education.

For Further Study (see resource list):

Noebel, David A. *Understanding the Times.*

Lesson 1

Defining Worldview

Life on Earth Is a Worldview War

Life on earth is a worldview war. In recent years, more and more Christian leaders are speaking to the church about this reality. Dr. James Dobson spoke about this conflict in 1990 in his book, *Children at Risk.*

"Nothing short of a great Civil War of Values rages today throughout North America. Two sides with vastly differing and incompatible worldviews are locked in a bitter conflict that permeates every level of society. Instead of fighting for territory or military conquest, however, the struggle now is for the hearts and minds of the people. It is a war over ideas. And someday soon, I believe, a winner will emerge, and the loser will fade from memory. For now, the outcome is very much in doubt.

On one side of this Continental Divide are the traditionalists whose values begin with the basic assumption that 'God is.' From that understanding comes a far-reaching system of thought that touches every dimension of life. Their beliefs are deeply rooted in the Ten Commandments and continuing through the New Testament teachings and gospel of Jesus Christ. Then, slowly at first, another way of looking at the world began to emerge. It evolved from the basic assumption that 'God isn't.' Everything emanating from the Creator was jettisoned, including reverence for the Scripture or any of the transcendent, universal truths. 'Right' was determined by what seemed right at a particular time."[1]

Some of the hard-core enemies of Christianity have understood the reality of this war long before Christians began to wake up to the fact. This article appeared in *The Humanist* magazine back in 1983.

"The Bible is not merely another book, an outmoded and archaic book, or even an extremely influential book. It has been and remains an incredibly dangerous book. It and the various Christian churches, which are parasitic upon it, have been directly responsible for most of the wars, persecutions, and outrages which humankind has perpetrated upon itself over the past thousand years--, I am convinced the battle for humankind's future must be waged and won in the public classroom by teachers who correctly perceive their roles as the proselytizers of a new faith. These teachers must embody the same dedication as the most rabid fundamentalist preachers, for they will be ministers of another sort, utilizing a classroom instead of a pulpit to convey humanist values in whatever subject they teach--- The classroom must and will become an arena of conflict between the old and the new—the rotting corpse of Christianity, together with all its adjacent evils and misery, and the new faith of humanism, resplendent in its promise of a world in which the ever-realized Christian ideal of "love thy neighbor,' will finally be achieved."[2]

It is easy to detect the anti-Christian bitterness in this article. Most Christians would consider this writer as someone coming from a fringe minority point of view. Most attacks on Christianity are not so blunt. (However, they are increasingly becoming so.) They are usually more subtle. So subtle that many, if not most, Christians do not see the anti-Christian hostility when it is there.

---

[1] James Dobson and Gary L. Bauer, *Children at Risk* (Dallas: Word Publishing, 1990), 19-21.

[2] John Dunphy, *The Humanist Magazine*, Jan/Feb 1983.

Yet how "fringe" are his assumptions? How many Americans, including Christians, believe that Christianity has "been responsible for most of the wars, persecutions, and outrages which humankind has perpetrated upon itself over the past two thousand years?" How many Christians know that this statement is an outrageous falsehood? How many of us see the importance of setting the record straight?

As a twentieth and twenty-first century church we have been slow to wake up to the fact that the enemies of Christianity have been busy attacking Christianity and the biblical worldview for several generations. Some of the enemies of Christianity are very conscious and deliberate in their hostility. Others are enemies of Christianity by default. They are merely going along with cultural trends that may seem innocuous on the surface but are indeed anti-Christian at the root. Unfortunately, many Christians fall into this latter category. What we have failed to realize is the essential spiritual dimension of the conflict.

Issues like abortion and homosexual "rights" have been hotly disputed between liberal humanists and conservative Christians for decades. The conflict is easy to see on the level of human interaction. The visible dispute is in the realm of words and actions which are based upon cherished values and opinions.

What is often overlooked is the fact that values are based upon basic beliefs and assumptions. These basic assumptions make up what we call a worldview. Some people are very conscious of their worldview and its ultimate source. Most people are controlled by a worldview that they have never really examined. They may not even be aware that they have a worldview. The truth is that every human being operates out of a worldview, whether he is conscious of it or not. One of the best definitions of worldview is the following.

"A worldview is a set of presuppositions (assumptions which may be true, partially true, or entirely false) which we hold (consciously or subconsciously, consistently or inconsistently) about the basic makeup of the world."[3]

---

[3] James W. Sire, *The Universe Next Door: A Basic Worldview Catalog, 3rd ed.* (Downers Grove, IL: InterVarsity Press, 1997), 17-18, quoted in Gary DeMar, *Thinking Straight in A Crooked World* (Powder Springs, GA: American Vision, 2001), 39.

What is a worldview?

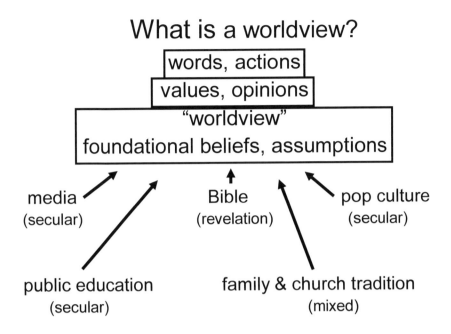

A Person's Worldview Governs the Way He Thinks

From where does our worldview, our set of basic beliefs and assumptions, come? The sources can be many and diverse. A few of the more influential sources of worldview are popular culture, the media, family and church tradition, and public education. These forces have varying degrees of impact on each individual's formation of his worldview. Ultimately these sources contain either truth or error, depending on whether they agree with the Word of God or disagree with it. In the real world, only the Bible is pure truth. All other sources are a mixture of truth and error. In modern America most of these other sources have become dominated by secular (godless) influences.

The point to remember is that everyone has a worldview, and that a person's worldview governs the way he thinks about every area of life. According to the apostle, Paul, Christian believers can come under the influence of unchristian thinking. He was speaking to believers in Colossians 2:8 when he said, *"Beware lest any man spoil you through philosophy and vain deceit, after the tradition of men, after the rudiments of the world, and not after Christ."*

The Advantage of Revelation

Francis Bacon (1561-1626), pioneer of the scientific method, said, "There are two books laid out before us to study, to prevent our falling into error; first, the volume of the Scriptures, which reveal the will of God; then the volume of Creation, which expresses His power." The problem with man is that sin has not only broken his relationship of close direct communication with God (as Adam had in the garden), but sin also destroyed man's ability to read God's "second book" of nature. Sin, a problem in man's heart, has also affected man's mind. Romans 1: 18-21 says: *"For the wrath of God is revealed from heaven against all ungodliness and unrighteousness of men, who hold the truth in unrighteousness; Because that which may be known of God is manifest in them; for God hath showed it unto them. For the invisible things of him from the creation of the world are clearly seen, being understood by the things that are made, even his eternal power and Godhead; so that they are without excuse: Because that, when they knew God, they glorified him not as God, neither were thankful; but became vain in their imaginations, and their foolish heart was darkened."*

Man's wickedness has not only destroyed his ability to see God through creation, it destroyed man's ability to comprehend creation itself. One of the results of rejecting God is general ignorance. Sinless Adam and Eve were the most intelligent human beings ever to live. Primitive, barbaric, cultures are not early stages of the evolution of man; these cultures are the result of sin. "Because that, when they knew God, they glorified him not as God, neither were thankful; but became vain in their imaginations, and their foolish heart was darkened."

But Jesus Christ reversed all of this. Because of man's depravity, man could not come to the knowledge of God through his own effort. But God made provision. *"And the Word was made flesh, and dwelt among us,"* (John 1:14) enabling man to come to a right knowledge of God. Not only does Jesus enable us to come to a right knowledge of God, but this Word of God enables us to correctly comprehend creation. This tremendous blessing is the great "advantage of revelation."

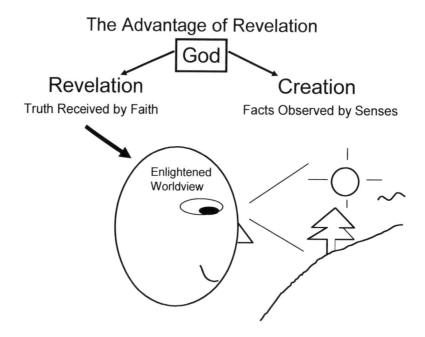

The Advantage of Revelation

God

Revelation
Truth Received by Faith

Creation
Facts Observed by Senses

Enlightened Worldview

The same God who created the universe wrote the Bible

The truth in the Bible, the revealed Word of God, gives us light for understanding in all areas of life. Some have seen the Bible as only a book of theology (the study of God). Indeed, it is the all-sufficient book of theology, but it is more. It is a book that enables us to understand God's creation. It contains principles that enable us to correctly understand philosophy, psychology, economics, politics, biology, and every other area of human study. The same God who wrote the Bible created the universe. As the saying goes, "For best results, follow the instructions of the maker." Biblical principles applied to life, all areas of life, work best in the real world. This is why nations that embrace Christianity prosper. As we shall see, all the blessings of liberty, prosperity, scientific technology, modern medicine and every blessing enjoyed by modern man, owe their existence to the application of principles found in the Bible.

It is extremely important to note, as the drawing shows, that this all begins by an act of faith. The Word of God is received by faith, not through an exercise of man's reasoning ability. Understanding, enlightenment, comes after faith. The Bible says that the fear of the Lord is the beginning of knowledge, understanding, and wisdom. Thus, the steps to success in understanding creation are as follows:

1. Receive the Word of God by faith.
2. Accept the Bible's view of everything.
3. This enables us to correctly interpret the facts we observe in the world.
4. Our conclusions based upon these interpretations will work in the real world.

Living in Darkness

What happens when men reject the truth of God is illustrated in the drawing below. Man can reject the truth of revelation. When he does, the result is personally tragic, for only through Jesus Christ may man receive eternal life. It also has its temporal consequences both for the individual and for society. Rejection of the truth produces a darkened worldview. The person who rejects the truth of the Bible will be unable to correctly interpret the phenomena he observes in this life. When he rejects God's truth, he has to invent a substitute explanation for what he observes in this world. Since his substitute worldview is in disagreement with the Creator's view, it is doomed to fail. This man's worldview will not work in the real world. The consequences are very real. When whole nations pursue policies that conflict with the Creator's worldview, the consequences can be catastrophic, as in the case of Nazi Germany or the Soviet Union.

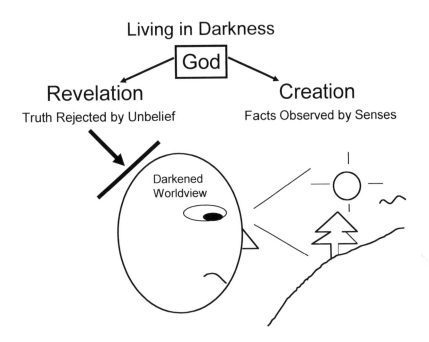

The man or the society that rejects revelation has guaranteed his own failure both on the eternal and on the temporal plain. Below are the steps to failure.

1. Reject the truth of revelation.
2. This necessitates inventing a substitute explanation for the facts observed by our senses.
3. Conclusions based upon these substitutions will not work in the real world.

Dangerous Substitutions

When man rejects God's explanation, he must invent a substitute worldview. The chart below lists some of the substitutions made by those who embrace a humanist philosophy of life. The quotes are taken from the Humanist Manifesto. The Humanist Manifesto (which we will study in more detail later) is a document that clearly states the humanist worldview. Although it was written by intellectuals and signed by men and women of academic and professional notoriety, it clearly expresses the worldview that dominates the thinking of our modern secular culture.

Rejected Biblical Truth

God Exists

"The fool hath said in his heart, 'There is no God'."
(Psalms 14:1)

Only the Material Exists
(No Spiritual Reality)

"We find insufficient evidence for belief in the existence of a supernatural; it is either meaningless or irrelevant to the question of the survival of the human race. As non-theists, we begin with humans not God, nature not deity."
(Humanist Manifesto II)

God Created the World

"In the beginning God created the heaven and the earth."
(Genesis 1:1)

Evolution

"Religious humanists regard the universe as self-existing and not created--- Humanism believes that man is part of nature and that he has emerged as the result of a continuous process."
(Humanist Manifesto I)

Sinful Nature of Man
"For all have sinned, and come short of the glory of God;"
(Romans 3:23)

Goodness (Perfectibility) of Man

"So stand the theses of religious humanism. Though we consider the religious forms and ideas of our fathers no longer adequate, the quest for the good life is still the central task of mankind. Man is at last becoming aware that he alone is responsible for the realization of the world of his dreams, that he has within himself the power for its achievement. He must set intelligence and will to the task.
(Humanist Manifesto I)

15

Substitute Humanistic Error

It is a big mistake to think of the academic or intellectual realm as having little or no effect on everyday life. This has been a serious shortcoming of the twentieth century church. For over 150 years we have abdicated our responsibility to speak truth in the intellectual and academic realm. This is a relatively new trend in the history of Christianity. Historically Christianity has been the leading influence in intellectual and academic affairs. When Christians fail to speak truth against errors like those expressed in the Humanist Manifesto, we are allowing these lies to advance and infect our culture.

When believers retreat from the intellectual realm and fail to confront error with truth, the consequences can be catastrophic. The "substituted humanist errors" on the right side of the chart are foundational to Marxism which is responsible for the deaths of countless millions of people in the twentieth century. Ideas have consequences. According to an extensive study, in the twentieth century alone over 170 million people were put to death by governments based upon worldviews that reject the truth of the Bible.[4] How many of these 170 million people died before they had the opportunity to hear the gospel? The same worldview that allowed these governments to slaughter their own people allowed them to persecute Christians and prohibit missionary activity in their countries.

And all we have to do is speak the truth. God is not asking us to confront with physical force. *"For the weapons of our warfare are not carnal, but mighty through God to the pulling down of strong holds; Casting down imaginations, and every high thing that exalteth itself against the knowledge of God and bringing into captivity every thought to the obedience of Christ;"* (II Corinthians 10: 4-5).

Some of the "dangerous substitutions" are very subtle and slow to infect society. They may not be the direct cause of the violent death of millions, but their consequences can be extremely destructive and far-reaching.

Consider the biblical truth that man is by nature prone to sin. The substitute belief that man is basically good is the foundation for practically every modern theory of human behavior. Virtually all secular psychology is based on this belief. It dominates contemporary thinking in education, parenting and counseling. Is there any wonder we have more problems with divorce, suicide, mental illness, attention deficit disorder, homosexuality, alcoholism, drug abuse, and illegitimate birth than at any other time in the history of our nation? We are building our social structure on erroneous assumptions about the nature of man. And in recent generations the Church has followed the secular culture down this slippery slope. We have been taking our philosophy of counseling, parenting, and education from the world instead of the Bible. This is why there are negligible differences between Christians and non-Christian Americans in the social statistics on divorce, alcoholism, and similar issues.

Worldview and Education

Different worldviews produce different results. God's way is the right way. He defines "right." Any way in conflict with God's way is a wrong way. It behooves us as Christian educators to seek the mind of God on the subject of teaching and learning. Too often we accept the teaching of the "experts" in education without examining their basic assumptions. No one person has had greater impact on modern American education than John Dewey. John Dewey was an atheistic secular humanist. His worldview, which determined his philosophy of education, was in direct conflict with the Bible. In past eras

---

[4] R.J. Rummel, *Death by Government* (New Brunswick: Transaction Publishers, 1994), 4.

16

Christian intellectuals would have contested Dewey's views. Today we teach his views in education classes in Christian colleges. Perhaps we should ask as the writer of the epistle did, *"Doth a fountain send forth at the same place sweet water and bitter?"* (James 3:11).

Some would say that an individual's religious beliefs are personal and do not affect his professional life. Atheistic doctors, for example, can effectively bring healing through surgery regardless of their worldview. Not so. Atheist or not, a doctor using modern medical science is working from a biblical, not an atheistic worldview. Modern medical science owes it existence to the biblical worldview. We will study this in more detail later. An atheistic surgeon is acting inconsistently with his religious assumptions when he practices the modern science of medicine.

John Dewey, however, was not inconsistent in his worldview when it came to education. He was a humanist all the way. As Christian educators we must examine the assumptions of those who teach and write about education because a person's worldview determines his philosophy of education, and a wrong worldview means wrong education.

Wrong Worldview Means Wrong Education

	Critical Questions	**Humanist Position**	**Christian Position**
Theology	Does God exist? Who is God? How does he reveal himself?	God does not exist.	God exists. Jesus is the Son of God. The Bible is revelation.
Philosophy of man	What is man?	Man is an accident of evolution. Man is his own redeemer. Collectively man determines all values.	Man is created by God and is subject to Him. God determines all values.
Philosophy of education	Why teach?	To equip the young to function as productive members of society.	To equip the young to give glory to God.
	What do we teach? (content)	Determined by society to serve its own purposes.	Whatever is needed to fulfill man's purpose as indicated in the Bible.
	How do we teach? (methods)	Man is an animal. Control his environment.	Man is created in the image of God. Impart truth

Note that the most crucial question is about the existence and identity of God. When a person answers the theological questions incorrectly, he must invent his own answers to the question, "What is man?" His philosophy of education will be based upon his erroneous understanding of the nature of man. The Christian believer, on the other hand, starts from the premise that the Bible reveals the mind of God. He does not have to invent a philosophy of man because the Bible tells him what man is. Furthermore, the Bible tells him why he should teach his children, what he should teach them, and (importantly) how he should teach them.

Christians might wonder what could be harmful about the humanist answers to the questions about why we teach, what we teach, and how we teach. After all, what is wrong with wanting young people to function as productive members of society? Does not the Bible exhort us to be good and peaceful citizens?

The problem is in the all-encompassing emphasis of the humanist on "society." For the godless humanist, society is the highest authority. But as Christians we belong to Christ. Our role in life is to give glory to God, not society. In the Bible we are admonished to live peaceful lives so that God will get the glory. Good citizenship is a means, not an end in itself. The role of education is to equip the young to give glory to God. The subtle and hostile agenda at the heart of humanistic education is to give glory to man and deny it to God. Furthermore, when we think of society as it applies to contemporary America, we think of institutions that still hold some values consistent with the Bible. But what happens to the concept of good citizenship when it applies to Soviet Russia or Nazi Germany? The problem lies in the fact that whenever God is removed from education, all education becomes a tool of whatever political group controls society. In contemporary America the control of education has slipped out from under those that hold a biblical worldview and into the hands of those who hold a humanist, therefore anti-Christian, worldview.

Defining Christian Education

Teachers, including Christian educators, tend to be eclectic in their choices of materials and methods they use in the classroom. They often make choices without reflecting on the philosophy of education on which the material or method is based. Many times it is difficult to discover the basic philosophy of the author of the material or method. Philosophical statements tend to be brief and sketchy if they even appear in the materials published today. As a result, many educational methods and materials based upon philosophies hostile to biblical thinking have crept into "Christian" education. It has gotten to the level that one could say that much of the education that takes place in a "Christian" school is not really Christian. Perhaps we need to more precisely define our terms. It is time we took a little quiz on Christian education.

<u>**Quiz on Christian Education**</u>

Which of the following elements make education "Christian"?

_____ Christian students
_____ Christian books and materials
_____ Christian church sponsors
_____ Christian teachers
_____ All of the above
_____ None of the above

The correct answer is "none of the above." We can have a school where all the students are personally committed to Jesus Christ. In that school we can use exclusively books and materials that are produced by Christian publishers. The school can be sponsored by a solid bible-believing Christian church. All the teachers in the school can be believers in Jesus Christ. Yet none of these factors guarantees that the education process will be Christian. If the educators in this school are following a philosophy or methodology that is based on any worldview other than the biblical worldview, the education process will not be Christian. To the degree education is governed by biblical principles it can rightly be labeled "Christian." Therefore, our definition of Christian education should be:

Christian education is education governed by biblical principles.

This means that many well-meaning Christian teachers could be participating in unchristian education. This is a fact. When it comes to education (not to mention parenting and "Christian" counseling) many of us are "functional humanists." A "functional humanist" is a person who unintentionally serves a humanist worldview in any given area. This is to be distinguished from a "conscious humanist" who is aware of his basic assumptions and is deliberately consistent in his worldview. Worldview inconsistency is a big problem among Christians.

Dr. David Noebel of Summit Ministries has constructed a worldview chart that lists the logically consistent positions of the major worldviews for various areas of study. For example, to be logically consistent with what the Bible says about economics, a person who accepts the biblical worldview should conclude that the bible supports the concept of private property or as Dr. Noebel labels it, "Stewardship of Property." In other words, a secular humanist that believes in socialism is consistent in his worldview. A Christian who believes in socialism is inconsistent in his worldview. In economics this Christian would be a "functional humanist."

In past centuries Christians have been much more consistent in their worldview. One of the major problems in the Church today is worldview inconsistency. Whose job is it to fix this? As Christian educators we could not live in a more challenging day and age than today.

Lesson 2

Humanism: The anti-Christian Worldview

Goals:

1. To gain a deeper understanding of what humanism is.
2. To gain a deeper appreciation of the spiritual significance of the worldview conflict.
3. To gain a deeper awareness of the hostility of humanism toward Christianity.
4. To gain a deeper understanding of the historical conflict between humanism and Christianity throughout the ages.

Assignment:

1. Read Lesson 2.
2. Write answers to Study Questions below.

Study Questions:

1. Explain how humanism is essentially the same sin Adam committed in the garden.
2. Explain how the cultural war is essentially spiritual.
3. List at least six ways humanism is anti-biblical.
4. Why is there no neutral ground in the worldview war?
5. Early church theologian Tertullian asked, "What has Athens to do with Jerusalem?" What is the significance of his famous question?
6. How is Hegel's theory of history anti-biblical?
7. Why are attempts to synthesize Christianity and humanism dangerous?

For Further Study (see resource list):

Kurtz, Paul (editor). *Humanist Manifestos I and II.* Buffalo: Prometheus Books, 1973.

Schaeffer, Francis A. *How Should We Then Live?* Wheaton, IL: Crossway Books, 1976.

Lesson 2

Humanism: The Anti-Christian Worldview

"Humanism, humanism, I'm tired of hearing about humanism!" This was the complaint of a teacher back in the late 1970's when she learned that the school board at her Christian school recommended that the faculty take time to study humanism. She expressed an opinion that was held by a large portion of the church, and that was almost thirty years ago. That attitude is just as strong today, and perhaps even more so. We can say this based upon the fact that in the intervening years it has been humanism and not Christianity that has had greater influence on American culture. Humanism has not only been the dominating influence on American culture, it has had great influence on the church. The process has been reversed. Whereas during the first three centuries of American history, Christianity was the dominant influence, in this last century humanism has emerged as the stronger influence. Now instead of the church influencing the culture, the culture is influencing the church.

Why is this? Has the power of untruth gotten stronger than the power of truth? Has the Word of God lost its power? Or are Christians failing to use the Word of God? We contend that the answer lies in the failure of Christians to know the Word of God and to speak the Word of God to the world.

Gary DeMar, President, American Vision, has an interesting way to illustrate this point through a "modern parable" he tells. It goes like this. A man is accosted by a mugger with a knife on a dark, deserted street. The man himself is armed with a .45 service automatic handgun. But notice what happens in the first instance:

"You (the man with the gun) shout to him (the mugger) in a weakened voice, 'Stop! If you take one more step I'll shoot!' (The mugger) laughs. Your seemingly calm demeanor turns to panic. Fear descends on you like a thick cloud. His mocking response sends an unfamiliar chill over you. 'I don't believe in guns,' he mutters. 'And I certainly don't believe in .45 service automatics.'

His words startle you. Fear has now gripped you like a vise. You're confused. Your shooting instructor never covered this situation. You put the gun down and allow the brute to slash you to pieces."[5]

DeMar repeats his parable with a different twist. In the second instance the scene is the same with the mugger threatening to attack with his knife:

"You (the man with the gun) realize that he (the mugger) wants to slash you to pieces. You remain calm. You pull out your .45 service automatic and point it at the attacker. You shout to him in a confident voice, 'Stop! If you take one more step, I'll shoot!' He laughs. He shouts back to you, "I don't believe in guns. And I certainly don't believe in .45 service automatics.' With that last word he lunges at you with death in his eyes. You make a believer out of him by emptying the clip of bullets into his lunging body."[6]

---

[5] Gary Demar, *Thinking Straight in a Crooked World* (Powder Springs, GA: American Vision, 2001), 4.
[6] Ibid.

21

In the Bible, the Word of God is compared to a sword. It is a spiritual weapon. It is a spiritual weapon that the modern American church seems reluctant to use. Just like the mugger in the story, modern secular man does not believe in swords. But as the story cleverly illustrates, the mugger's lack of belief in the power of .45 service automatics did not change the gun's effectiveness.

Martin Luther once said that the man who fails to stand up for biblical truth on the particular point that is being attacked becomes a denier of the faith:

> "If I profess with the loudest voice and clearest exposition every portion of the truth of God except precisely that little point which the world and devil are at that moment attacking, I am not confessing Christ, however boldly I may be professing Christ. Where the battle rages, there the loyalty of the soldier is proved and to be steady on all the battlefields besides is mere flight and disgrace if he flinches at that one point."[7]

The modern American church seems to have lost its stomach to stand up for truth. We have become desensitized toward humanism. We not only accommodate it, we have embraced it. The book of Hebrews urges us not to grow weary in our struggle against sin. We need to recognize humanism for what it really is. Humanism is sin.

Humanism: The Original Sin

Humanism is the basic sin of man wanting life without God. It is the rejection of God and the exaltation of man. It is the beginning point of all man's troubles. It is the original sin of Adam in the garden. Although we could not call Adam a humanist, he committed the humanist sin. He gave in to the temptation to eat from the tree of the knowledge of good and evil. This was the great act of rebellion. Man wanted to throw off God's rules and determine what was good and evil for himself.

It is crucial to the study of humanism to keep in mind that at its root is rebellion. It is therefore objectively evil. It carries in it hostility toward God. God had declared that tree to be "off limits." Adam's decision ran contrary to God's will. Every thought based upon the rejection of God is hostile toward God. Humanism as a worldview is a whole system of thinking based upon the rejection of God. It carries in it an anti-God agenda. This anti-god agenda comes from the one who tempted Adam in the first place—the serpent.

When we look at it this way, we should have a better understanding of the so-called "cultural war" in our nation today. The conflicts we see on the nightly news are merely the superficial acting out of a deeper spiritual war. There are levels of warfare of which human interaction is only the surface level. As we have discussed, men's actions are determined by their values, which are determined by their basic assumptions (their worldview). But there is an underlying spiritual war that feeds and fuels hostility toward God. This is the spiritual level.

---

[7] Martin Luther, quoted in William J. Federer, ed.., *America's God and Country Encyclopedia of Quotations* (Coppell, TX: Fame Pub., 1994), 404.

Levels of Warfare

Humanism   vs.   Christianity

Human Interaction Level

liberal politics	"religious right"
humanistic education	biblical education

Intellectual Level

humanism	biblical worldview

Spiritual Level

Satan's rage	God's holiness

In its generic form, humanism is the mother of all anti-Christian philosophies. The ancient Greek philosophers were the first humanists in the sense that they rejected all ideas of any kind of god. About 600 BC the philosopher, Thales, known as the "Father of Western Philosophy," began to teach that there were no supernatural beings. This was the beginning of secular thinking. (It is interesting that Thales's follower, Anaximander, developed the first theory of evolution.)

Over the centuries humanism has taken on a variety of forms. At various times in history and in different parts of the world, humanism has exerted its anti-Christian influence. For example, Dr. Noebel's chart names three modern forms: secular humanism, Marxism/Leninism, and "cosmic humanism." Although all three forms, as well as other anti-Christian worldviews, have strong influence on modern American culture, we will turn our attention specifically to secular humanism which still is the strongest anti-Christian influence in America today. Specifically, we will study the Humanist Manifestos. Keep in mind that there is much common belief among the different brands of humanism. The Humanist Manifestos, for example, contain the basic beliefs of both secular humanism and Marxism.

The Humanist Manifestos

The vast majority of Americans, including those that would even call themselves humanists, do not know that the Humanist Manifestos even exist. Why then, should we take time to study these dusty, old, boring documents? After all, only a tiny percentage of Americans ever read those things. Aren't these matters for the intellectual elite?

Although only a small intellectual elite signed these documents, the Manifestos contain the basic beliefs that are espoused by most Americans today. As we pointed out earlier, most people do not even know they have a worldview, but if they could go deep down into their basic assumptions, they would discover the Humanist Manifestos.

Humanist Manifesto I was written in 1933. It was signed by thirty-four influential professionals and intellectuals. Notable among them is John Dewey, the father of modern secular education. The second Manifesto was drafted forty years later. Over 250 signed Humanist Manifesto II. Among signers are numerous writers, university professors, and activists who have had tremendous impact on modern America. They include: Betty Friedan, leader of the modern feminist movement and founder of the National Organization of Women; Alan Guttmacher, pro-abortion activist and president of Planned Parenthood Federation of America; B.F. Skinner, Harvard professor of psychology who is the father of behavior modification and has had enormous influence on modern psychology; Sir Julian Huxley, former head of UNESCO; and several very influential writers including Isaac Asimov and Gunnar Myrdal.

As we examine several quotes from Humanist Manifestos I and II, note the hostility toward Christianity. There is no neutrality when it comes to worldview.

Humanism Is Atheistic

"As in 1933, humanists still believe that traditional theism, especially faith in the prayer-hearing God, assumed to love and care for persons, to hear and understand their prayers, and to be able to do something about them, is an unproved and outmoded faith."[8]

"We believe, however, that traditional dogmatic or authoritarian religions that place revelation, God, ritual, or creed above human needs and experience do a disservice to the human species."[9]

"We find insufficient evidence for belief in the existence of a supernatural; it is either meaningless or irrelevant to the question of the survival and fulfillment of the human race. As non-theists, we begin with humans not God, nature not deity."[10]

"Promises of immortal salvation or fear of eternal damnation are both illusory and harmful. They distract humans from present concerns, from self-actualization, and from rectifying social injustices."[11]

Humanism Is Man-centered

"Religious humanism considers the complete realization of human personality to be the end of man's life and seeks its development and fulfillment in the here and now. This is the explanation of the humanist's social passion."[12]

"Religious humanism maintains that all associations and institutions exist for the fulfillment of human life."[13]

Humanism Firmly Believes in Evolution

"First: Religious humanists regard the universe as self-existing and not created."[14]

"Humanism believes that man is part of nature and that he has emerged as the result of a continuous process."[15]

---

[8] Paul Kurtz, ed., *Humanist Manifestos I and II* (Buffalo: Prometheus Books, 1973), 13.
[9] Ibid., 15-16.
[10] Ibid., 16.
[11] Ibid.
[12] Ibid., 9.
[13] Ibid.
[14] Ibid., 8.
[15] Ibid.

Humanism Believes in Moral Relativism

"Humanism asserts that the nature of the universe depicted by modern science makes unacceptable any supernatural or cosmic guarantees of human values."[16]

"We affirm that moral values derive their source from human experience. Ethics is autonomous and situational, needing no theological or ideological sanction."[17]

Humanism Is Socialistic

"The humanists are firmly convinced that existing acquisitive and profit-motivated society has shown itself to be inadequate and that a radical change in methods, controls, and motives must be instituted. A socialized and cooperative economic order must be established to the end that equitable distribution of the means of life be possible."[18]

Humanism Believes in Global Government

"We deplore the division of humankind on nationalistic grounds. We have reached a turning point in history where the best option is to transcend the limits of national sovereignty and to move toward the building of a world community in which all sectors of the human family can participate. Thus we look to the development of a system of world law and a world order based upon transnational federal government."[19]

Humanism Promotes Sexual "Freedom"

"In the area of sexuality, we believe that intolerant attitudes, often cultivated by orthodox religions and puritanical cultures, unduly repress sexual conduct. The right to birth control, abortion, and divorce should be recognized. While we do not approve of exploitive, denigrating forms of sexual expression, neither do we wish to prohibit, by law or social sanction, sexual behavior between consenting adults. The many verities of sexual exploration should not in themselves be considered 'evil'."[20]

Humanism Promotes the "Right" to Die

"It also includes recognition of an individual's right to die with dignity, euthanasia, and the right to suicide."[21]

Humanism Summed Up

"So stand the theses of religious humanism. Though we consider the religious forms and ideas of our fathers no longer adequate, the quest for the good life is still the central task for mankind. Man is at last becoming aware that he alone is responsible for the realization of the world of his dreams, that he has within himself the power for its achievement. He must set intelligence and will to the task."[22]

The Humanist Manifestos present humanism in the raw. In everyday life we usually do not encounter humanism in such concise philosophical statements. In contemporary culture it tends to live below the surface of consciousness in most people's thinking. Yet it is there in all its hostility toward God and Christianity.

---

[16] Ibid.
[17] Ibid., 17.
[18] Ibid., 10.
[19] Ibid., 21.
[20] Ibid., 18.
[21] Ibid., 19.
[22] Ibid., 10.

The Conflict of the Ages

In this course we will be using the term "humanism" in its generic sense. Throughout history humanism has taken a variety of forms and expressions. In all these expressions there is a common theme. This common ground is a rejection of God and an exaltation of man.

Eden was the birthplace of humanism. From there we can trace humanistic hostility toward God throughout history. Some of the major historical expressions of humanism are shown on the left side of the chart below. Listed on the right side are some of the major historical expressions of the opposing biblical worldview. Dates given are approximate.

The Conflict of the Ages

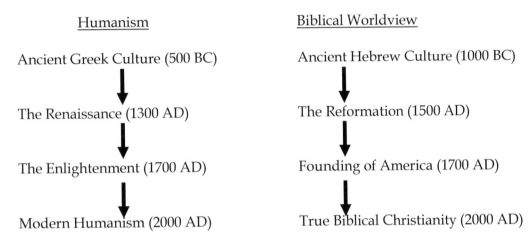

Humanism	Biblical Worldview
Ancient Greek Culture (500 BC)	Ancient Hebrew Culture (1000 BC)
The Renaissance (1300 AD)	The Reformation (1500 AD)
The Enlightenment (1700 AD)	Founding of America (1700 AD)
Modern Humanism (2000 AD)	True Biblical Christianity (2000 AD)

Note that the above chart is meant only to give a general overview of some of the major historical expressions of these conflicting worldviews. It is beyond the scope of this course to examine them in detail. The study of history from this perspective is very important to developing a biblical worldview. We believe it should be part of every teacher's academic background. Unfortunately, very few Christian colleges present history from this perspective. Please refer to our resource list for titles of books on this subject. We highly recommend reading *How Shall We Then Live* by Francis Schaeffer.

The two ancient cultures that best expressed this contrast in worldview were the Greeks and the Hebrews. The culture of ancient Greece was basically the highest and purest expression of self-conscious humanism to appear to date in the history of man. Secular historians present ancient Greece as the birthplace of human rights, democracy, and just about everything "good" about Western civilization. These historians claim that America owes its high level of liberty to ideas about government that came from the ancient Greeks. Most Christians accept this erroneous secular view of history.

The truth is that Greek ideas of government were based upon a humanistic worldview. This view made man the highest authority. America was founded upon the biblical worldview which accepted God as the highest authority. We will consider this point in more detail shortly. Our point for now is that ancient Greek culture was a major expression of the humanistic worldview, and contrary to the reports of the secular historians, ancient Greece's contribution to Western civilization was more negative than positive. For more information on this subject read *What If Jesus Had Never Been Born* by Dr. D. James Kennedy.

On the other hand, ancient Hebrew culture was the best expression to date of a culture based upon biblical truth. The Hebrew culture was God-centered. This is not to say that every Hebrew followed God's commandments faithfully. On the contrary, the Bible tells us they were often unfaithful. But in spite of their shortcomings, the Hebrews were the best example to date in history of a culture based upon the Bible. The Hebrew worldview was in stark contrast to the humanistic worldview of the ancient Greeks. This is seen in the completely different views each culture had on family, education, government and a host of other subjects.

Christianity took up where the Hebrews left off. With the light of the New Testament, early Christians developed a culture with an even clearer biblical worldview than their predecessors.

As Christianity spread into Europe and became the dominant religion, the biblical worldview gained influence on the cultures of the continent. This is not to say that humanistic and pagan influence was eliminated. To the contrary, often the beliefs of Christianity became mixed with humanistic and pagan beliefs. The result was a worldview that was not a pure biblical worldview. For example, the Roman Catholic Church retained a pagan view of government. However, it is accurate to say that the overall influence of Christianity was to replace the humanistic and pagan worldviews with a generally God-centered worldview.

With the Renaissance came a great revival of humanism. During the Renaissance intellectuals and artists rediscovered the "glory that was Greece" along with its infatuation with humanity. Although the Renaissance maintained an outward regard for Christian tradition, at its core was affection for humanism. Francis Schaeffer points out that although the subject of Renaissance artists and writers was usually religious, their thought was often humanistic.

The Reformation was the great reawakening of the biblical worldview. With its emphasis on the authority of the Bible and the importance of every man reading the Word of God for himself, men developed a renewed respect for biblical truth. A fresh love for truth and recognition that the Bible provides truth for all of life fostered the development of a much more clearly biblical worldview than European Christians had ever previously held. The true source of the early American concepts of government and education can be traced to the Reformation.

The Enlightenment of the eighteenth century was an outbreak of militant anti-Christian humanism. It provided the philosophy that under-girded the bloody French Revolution. On the other hand, the biblical worldview found great expression in the founding of America, a nation based more upon biblical principles of government than any other since the ancient Hebrews.

Comparing the French Revolution with the American Revolution sheds much light on the difference between the humanistic and the biblical worldview. The French Revolution's Declaration of the Rights of Man is often erroneously presented as a European version of the American Declaration of Independence. This is far from the truth.

The American Declaration of Independence is based upon the biblical worldview. Man's "inalienable rights" are endowed by the "Creator." America was founded upon the biblical idea that God gives rights, not human governments. And America was founded upon the concept of government run by men who are submitted to the law of God. This is what we mean when we say America was founded as a Christian nation. The predominant view of government of our founders was the biblical worldview, not the humanistic thinking of the Enlightenment or the ancient Greeks. The liberty we enjoy comes from founding our government upon a biblical worldview. It is extremely important that Christians, especially Christian educators understand this issue. Please refer to our resource list for several titles that deal with this issue.

The French Revolution, on the other hand, was founded on the humanistic thinking of the Enlightenment. There is no recognition of the supremacy of God in the French Declaration of the Rights of Man. The French Revolution was purely humanistic. It was based upon the idea of the supremacy of man.

History reveals the fruit of worldviews. The humanistic French Revolution resulted in anarchy, the bloody reign of terror, and tyrannical dictatorship. Since the French Revolution, France has changed its form of government and written new constitutions many times. On the other hand, the American Revolution created the nation that has provided the most liberty, security, and prosperity of any government to date in history.

Today we see the same war of worldviews raging in modern America. As mentioned earlier, the political, social, educational and cultural conflicts in our nation today are outward expressions of the conflict between the humanistic and the biblical worldviews.

Below is a fascinating chart showing the gradual but effective transition from an essentially biblical worldview of life embraced by the Puritans to an essentially humanistic worldview of life embraced by the public square in America today.

The History of American Education/Culture

Developed by:
Dr. Gerald Stiles
Liberty University

	I. Colonial Education Era	II. Early National Era	III. State School Era	IV. Remaking of Society Era	V. Post-Christian Era	VI. New World Order Era
Character:	CHRISTIANIZATION	NATIONALIZATION	AMERICANIZATION	DEMOCRATIZATION	INDIVIDUALIZATION	RECULTURIZATION
Period:	(1620 - 1776)	(1789 - 1840)	(1840 - 1918)	(1918 - 1963)	(1963 - 1993)	(1993 - ?)
What is real	1. GOD 2. CHRIST	1. GOD 2. CHRIST 3. SCIENCE	SCIENCE / GOD	1. SCIENCE 2. GOD	1. SCIENCE 2. NEW AGE	1. NEW AGE 2. SCIENCE
How we know what we know	1. BIBLE 2. REASON	BIBLE / REASON	1. REASON 2. BIBLE 3. INDV. DESIRES	1. REASON 2. INDV. DESIRES 3. BIBLE	1. INDV. DESIRES 2. REASON 3. EXPERIENCE	1. EXPERIENCE 2. INDV. DESIRES
Demonstration of, 'good life'	CHRISTIAN LIFE	1. CHRISTIAN LIFE 2. GOOD CITIZENSHIP	1. GOOD CITIZENSHIP 2. CHRISTIAN LIFE	1. GOOD CITIZENSHIP 2. MORAL LIFE 3. SELF-ACTUALIZED LIFE	1. SELF-ACTUALIZATION 2. CITIZENSHIP 3. MORALITY	1. POLITICAL CORRECTNESS 2. "IMMORALITY"

This chart shows the gradual shift away from the Judeo-Christian ethic towards Socialism and New Age beliefs.

(Items listed in order of perceived priority)

Exhibit A

Notes for History of American Education/Culture Charts

Period I- 150 years

This covers the period from the landing of the Pilgrims and Puritans to the War of Independence. While not everyone was a Christian, it is clear from numerous sources that the dominate ethos of that time was based on the Christian life. People commonly referred to themselves as "Christians seeking the new city on a hill." Many Christian institutions were established including schools for higher education, Harvard, Yale, etc.

Period II- 50 years

We had now become a "nation" in our own right. People began to refer to themselves as 'the new nation' more than simply the people of God. Science became an acceptable way of knowing truth, though not equal with God and Christ. Reason was put on the same level as the Bible for how we know what we know. Being a 'good citizen' was deemed an acceptable condition for having the good life.

Period III- 80 years

People now were quick to identify themselves as Americans first, then Christian. Science was made equal with God in ability to determine what was real. The scientist could be trusted to 'tell the truth.' Reason was viewed as the primary means of determining what man could/should know. Being a 'good citizen' was considered as the first test of the good life, but the Christian life was still considered important.

Period IV- 50 years
People now began to think of themselves as belonging to a 'democracy,' rather than to a Constitutional Republic, as given by the Founding Fathers. This political mindset was based on an inerrant understanding of the phrase 'we the people' as used by the founding fathers. Man's will was made dominate rather than the will of God as expressed in Biblical law and constitutional law. This shift in political thinking laid the foundation for the 'me generation' which showed up in the next shift in culture, Period V. Reason and individual desires were viewed as the basis of what we know, more than the Bible. Being a good citizen, possessing a moral life, and embracing the "self-actualized life," (humanistic psychology) was the basis of having the 'good life.'

Period V- 30 years
A major shift was now underway in America. The "60's" kicked in and almost overnight people could sense a new day was dawning. Nearly everyone new that something was happening to America, few understood why. Even fewer understood the consequences of where this would lead our nation. One who did see the cause and the consequences was Francis Schaeffer. The adoption of 'we the people' politically led to the adoption of 'me the person' morally and culturally. The 'Me Generation' was in full bloom with youth expressing rebellion against traditional authority, particularly on the college campuses. Science along with "technological Eastern religion," called New Age, became the focus of what was real.   Individual desires, reason and experience were the dominate basis for determining what we can know.

Gone almost entirely was any public expression or acknowledgement of God, Christ, and the Bible. Christianity was at best 'one of many' views of life. Elvis Presley, the Beatles and the assassination of President Kennedy (all in the 60's) had a profound impact on the soul of America.

Period VI- underway
Postmodernism, a philosophy of the Enlightenment period in Europe, became the rage of the campuses in America. Objective truth was gone, man-made ethics was in. The church began mimicking the world more than confronting it. "Give them what they want" became the mantra for much of evangelicalism. The 'good life' was (and is!) characterized by a new virtue- tolerance. America adopted 'political correctness' as the basis for the good life, even respecting/promoting amoral behavior such as the gay lifestyle and now gay marriage in a few nations.

Given the history of our nation, especially in political and educational realms, we can now expect one of two 'characters' to develop.   It is near certain that we will either slide into barbarianism (as many cultures have done) or restore a thoroughly Biblically-based culture. Barbarianism is a topic of concern to many conservative evangelicals.   A good book on this subject is <u>Slouching Toward Gomorrah</u> by Thomas Bork.

Although uncertain as to when this may have begun, the cultural shift by youth into Humanism/Socialism as identified by Nehemiah Institute's PEERS Test, the trend of the past 18 years gives evidence that by 2020 (if trend continues at same rate) we will have a full generation of Americans who will strongly reject Christianity and formally embrace Socialism.

The direction we take will be largely determined by the church of our time. The under-shepherds (pastors of local churches) have an enormous task upon their shoulders.

Worldview Incompatibility

University professors of history have often portrayed the history of Western Civilization as the great civilization that stands on the twin pillars of ancient Greece and biblical Christianity. The implication is that we moderns owe an equal debt to both the Greeks and the Hebrews for the high level of civilization we enjoy today. (In recent generations the emphasis has changed to the positive influence of Greece, while Christianity's influence is portrayed as negative). The "twin pillar" view creates the impression that both ancient Greece and biblical Christianity were equally positive influences on the development of Western Civilization. While it is true that both have had tremendous influence on the history of Western Civilization, it must be kept in mind that these were diametrically opposed worldviews.

The early church theologian Tertullian recognized this fact way back in the third century when he asked, "What has Athens to do with Jerusalem?" Both forces have shaped the culture of modern western man, but from opposing points of view in every area of thought. Only Christianity has the advantage of revelation. The "glory of ancient Greece" is wishful thinking on the part of men who have chosen to reject the truth of revelation and rely on human speculation.

There is an erroneous and unbiblical way that we can view the contributions of both ancient Greece and biblical Christianity as both positive. We can subscribe to the philosophy of history developed by the eighteenth century German philosopher Georg Wilhelm Friedrich Hegel. Hegel's view was that history was a continuous process of development towards higher levels of civilization. His theory of the historical dialectic stated that for every idea or way of thinking (thesis) an opposing view would arise (antithesis). He believed that when these forces clashed and influenced each other, the result would be a third or new point of view (synthesis). This resulting synthesis would be superior to both the original thesis and antithesis. Thus upward progress was assured. The process was continuous because each synthesis would become the new thesis to in turn be challenged by a new antithesis, and the next process of reaching synthesis would begin. It can be diagramed to look like this.

Hegel's Dialectic

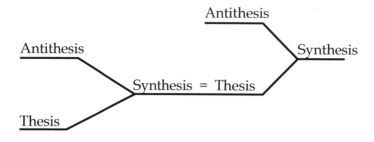

Hegel's view, however, is totally incompatible with biblical thinking. The Bible presents truth as immutable. The Word of God does not synthesize.

This however does not seem to keep Christians from trying to mix truth with error. Throughout history men have tried to synthesize biblical truth with the philosophies of men. In the middle ages, for instance, theologian Thomas Aquinas attempted to reconcile the philosophy of Aristotle with the Bible. The result became known as Scholasticism. Aquinas probably never anticipated the problems his work would cause to future generations.

Scholasticism was an attempt to synthesize the Greek mentality with the Hebrew mentality. For the Greeks, man was the focal point, and human reason was the path to "truth." God was the focal point in the Hebrew mentality and revelation was the path to truth. Scholasticism suggested that man could come to a knowledge of God through human reason. This opened the door to the attitude that human reason was as reliable as revelation for coming to know truth. Humanism had gained a foothold in the church.

The result of Scholasticism was a subtle erosion of confidence in revelation. This led to increased confidence in reaching truth by reason alone without the aid of revelation. At a time when the whole of western civilization looked to the Bible to shape its worldview, Aquinas open the door to the possibility of developing one's worldview independent of revelation.

Throughout the ages anti-Christian forces have caused confusion by attempting synthesis. Deism became popular during the eighteenth century Enlightenment. Deism was an attempt to mix Christian beliefs with a diminished concept of God. This view maintains a belief in a God who created the universe but this God remains aloof from the affairs of men. The Deistic idea of God is not biblical. The Bible clearly describes God as intimately involved in the affairs of men.

Deism was born out of a humanistic attitude of intellectual arrogance that viewed human reasoning as superior to submission to the authority of scripture and piety as sub-intellectual. This attitude fostered a false sense of separation between intellectual pursuit and Christian belief. Secular thinking received a significant boost from Deism which became a stepping-stone toward apostasy for much of western civilization.

Synthesizing biblical Christianity and humanism in America took the form of Unitarianism and Transcendentalism in the early nineteenth century. Again, an intellectual arrogance came into play. The Unitarians, like the Deists, looked down on Bible revering Christians as simplistic. They believed morality could be separated from religious piety and the Bible. They maintained a zeal for doing good but rejected the authority of the Word of God. As a result, they became America's original "do-gooders" who produced Horace Mann and the tradition that has led to the liberal social planners of modern politically correct America.

Synthesizing forces are at work in the church today. Many Christians want to find a way of peaceful coexistence with our humanistic culture. It cannot be done. True Christianity simply does not synthesize. God's Word does not compromise. It cannot be improved upon. Christianity and humanism are totally incompatible. Synthesis always results in compromising the Word of God, and Christians who try to do it get led astray.

The Christian who thinks he can peacefully coexist with humanism is a fool. This is the eternal truth about the conflict of the ages.

Lesson 3

The Humanistic versus the Biblical Tradition in Education

Goals:

1. To gain a deeper understanding of the philosophical conflict between biblical and humanistic education.
2. To gain historical perspective of the development of both the humanistic and the biblical philosophy of education.

Assignment:

1. Read Lesson 3.
2. Write answers to Study Questions below.

Study Questions:

1. What can we learn by comparing ancient Greek and Hebrew thinking about education?
2. Did the ancient Greeks appreciate reasoning more than the Hebrews? Why or why not?
3. Explain how each of the following contributed to the humanist tradition in education:
   a) the ancient Greeks
   b) Jean Jacques Rousseau
   c) Friedrich Froebel
4. Explain how each of the following contributed to the biblical tradition in education:
   a) the ancient Hebrews
   b) the Reformation
   c) the New England Puritans

For Further Study (see resource list):

Overman, Christian. *Assumptions That Affect Our Lives.* Louisiana, MO: Micah Publishing, 1996.

Barton, David. "Education and the Founding Fathers" (video). Aledo, TX: WallBuilders, 1993

Lesson 3

The Humanistic versus the Biblical Tradition in Education

Greek versus Hebrew Education

A major battlefront in the worldview war is in the arena of education. As noted earlier, one's philosophy of education is determined by one's basic assumptions about the existence of God, the nature of truth, and the nature of man. Thus, the two major worldviews, the God-centered biblical worldview and the man-centered humanistic worldview, have produced diametrically opposed philosophies of education. Again, we can go back to the ancient Greeks and Hebrews to see this contrast.

Society as understood by the Greek worldview did not encourage strong families, and education was for the elite few. Among the Hebrews education was important for everyone because it was intricately tied to their religion. Many passages in the Old Testament admonish fathers to raise their children according to God's ways. Fathers were told to teach, instruct, and impress upon their children God's truth. (See Deuteronomy 6:7). Modern words we could use here are "inculcate" or "indoctrinate." The fact that these words are politically incorrect terms today shows how far our cultural thinking about education has strayed from biblical thinking.

The chart below summarizes some of the basic differences between the Greek and the Hebrew concepts of education.

Greek	Hebrew
humanistic worldview	biblical worldview
man-centered	God-centered
Plato/Aristotle	Moses/Solomon
civic-centered	family-centered
education serves the state	education serves God
education is responsibility of state	education is responsibility of family
goal: good citizens	goal: godly character
focus on form (external)	focus on content (internal)
trust in human reason	trust in revelation
reason to "truth"	reason from Truth
	belief before understanding
man's autonomy	trust in authority
philosophic speculation	teach = instruct, inculcate
	memorize, meditate
	Word based
	importance of literacy

When the writings of the ancient Greeks, such as Plato and Aristotle, are compared to the Old Testament we see a stark contrast in their view of man. Lacking the truth of revelation, the Greeks had a thoroughly man-centered worldview. For these people, the temporal civic

34

society, or polis, was the highest expression of human life and achievement. Man was fulfilled through his identity with civic society. The Greek city-state was the highest authority and loyal citizenship was the highest virtue. Education's chief purpose was to produce civic virtue. Good, loyal citizens were the goal of Greek education, and education was the responsibility of the state.

Lacking knowledge of God and eternity, the Greek mind was stuck in the physical here and now. As a result Greek education and art concentrated upon physical form, especially the perfect human body. Style was important.

By contrast, the Hebrews took their cue from the Bible which concerned itself not with outward appearances but with what was in the heart of a man. The essence of a man was what is in his heart. The Bible does not dwell on physical appearance. The Bible is so unconcerned about physical appearance that you can find no physical descriptions of people in the scriptures except passing references that David was good looking, and Paul was not. We have no physical description of Jesus, for example. The Bible concentrates on the content of the heart of God and man. Thus developing godly character becomes the chief end of Hebrew education.

The most significant differences between Greek and Hebrew education have to do with the role of reason and revelation. As noted, the Greeks had no revelation. They believed man could reach truth through the process of reasoning alone. The starting point was the mind of autonomous man and the process was philosophic speculation. The Greeks believed man reasoned **to** truth.

It is amazing how one little preposition can mean so much, but the difference between reasoning **to** truth and reasoning **from** truth is immense. Whereas the Greeks tried in vain to reason to truth, the Hebrews had Truth as their starting point. For example, in the seventh century B.C., while Greek philosophers like Thales and Anaximenes were speculating that the earth evolved from water and air, the Hebrews had already possessed for centuries the truth about creation in the Book of Genesis.

The contrast between Greek and Hebrew thinking is often portrayed as the "conflict between reason and faith." This is an absolutely false portrayal. The Hebrews highly valued reason. They took their cue from Isaiah 1:18 which says, *"Come now, and let us reason together, saith the Lord."* The Hebrews understood that they were *"fearfully and wonderfully made"* (Psalm 139:14) and that God expected them to use their minds to know Him and understand His creation. Reason was very important to them, but it was not the starting point. Revelation was. The Hebrews began with Truth. They understood that the Word of God contains principles applicable to every area of life and that God gave us language and logic as a means to know Him and His truth. Logic was not Aristotle's invention; it was a gift from God to enable men to reason from revelation to practical life application. The Hebrews did not see reason in conflict with faith, but rather as a complement to faith.

Sometimes educators naively say, "All teaching methods are equal." Nothing could be further from the truth. Teaching methods are derived from one's philosophy of education. If the philosophy of education is based upon reality (a biblical worldview), its methods will be effective. If the philosophy of education is based upon error (any non-biblical worldview) its methods will fail to truly educate. The Hebrews saw the Bible as the model for teaching methods.

Revelation by definition is God speaking to man. If revelation is God's Word, it has authority. It is the highest authority. Accepting revelation means submitting to authority. The Hebrews understood that there is Authority above and outside of men. The Greeks did not recognize any authority above man. This difference in worldview had profound impact upon their concepts of education. Whereas the Hebrews trusted in the authority of revelation, the Greeks trusted in the autonomous reasoning power of man.

When it came to teaching methods, the Hebrews saw authority as integral to education. Learning began with acceptance of authority. Proverbs 1:7 states, *"The fear of the Lord is the beginning of knowledge."* Throughout Proverbs we see the picture of a father speaking and a son listening. *"My son, hear the instruction of thy father,"* says Proverbs 1:8. To the Hebrews education was primarily direct instruction. Today direct instruction is ridiculed as outmoded and ineffective by the modern education "experts."

If scripture is the written Word of God, learning to read becomes vital. Thus the Hebrews placed high value on literacy. In virtually every ancient pagan civilization literacy was limited to the priests and government officials. In ancient Greece schools were limited to those from the social class that controlled the government.

Memorization also is often criticized by modern secular educators, yet the Bible encourages us to take the truth to heart and meditate on it (See Psalms 1, 63, 77, 119, and Joshua 1:8).

We have used the ancient Greeks and Hebrews to illustrate this fundamental difference in philosophy and practice of education, but just as the conflict in worldview has continued throughout the ages, so has this conflict in education continued down to our present time. When humanism revived, as during the Enlightenment, humanistic educational practices were promoted. When the biblical worldview revived, as during the Reformation, biblical educational practices were promoted.

The Humanist Tradition in Education

Whereas the Renaissance was a revival of humanistic thought, it remained to a large degree ensconced in religious trappings. The Enlightenment, on the other hand, was more blatantly anti-Christian. Enlightenment thinking is the foundation of modern secularism, and one of its main spokesmen, Jean Jacques Rousseau, laid the foundations for modern secular education.

Rousseau

It is amazing that Jean Jacques Rousseau (1712-1778) could be held up as an authority on education when you consider his personal failure as a father. Rousseau begat five children by the same mistress whom he never married. All five children were taken as infants and abandoned at the Paris *Hopital des Enfants-Trouves*.[23] As a man, Rousseau has been described as highly emotional, erratic, paranoid, a creative genius and a reprobate. Rousseau never raised his own children. He never taught in a school. Yet his influence on modern man's thinking about education has been paramount. Rousseau's message was received and exalted because he spoke the message that God-rejecting men wanted to hear.

Rousseau in his theory of the "natural man" threw out the Bible's account of the fall and man's sinful nature. In his *Discourse of the Inequalities of Men* (1754) and *Social Contract* (1762) he maintained that man is essentially born good and is only corrupted by society. Since a child is born good, the best education is to allow the natural impulses and inclinations of the child to determine what he learns and when he learns it. Education for Rousseau was not imparting truth or knowledge to the child from outside sources. Outside sources, especially books, were the corrupting influences of society. The best education, as he described in his novel, *Emile*

---

[23] Paul Johnson, *Intellectuals* (New York: Harper & Row, 1988), 21.

(1762), is the drawing out of the natural goodness and primitive innocence that is already in a child.

Rousseau's influence on education grew in the generations after his death. As noted, he himself was not an educator, but others who were attracted to his humanistic worldview found ways to build a philosophy of education upon Rousseau's foundations.

Pestalozzi

Johann Heinrich Pestalozzi (1746-1827) was a Swiss educational reformer who developed and applied Rousseau's ideas. Pestalozzi was director of an experimental institute at Yverdon where Rousseau's philosophy of human nature was translated into teaching methods. He opposed verbalization, memorization, reading, and strict discipline. He believed showering children with affection would eliminate the need for discipline. Like Rousseau, he believed the child was the best determiner of what he should learn and when he should learn it. Pestalozzi was one of the pioneers in promoting the idea of "readiness." He believed the learning process should be based upon the natural inclinations of the child. He stressed the use of tactile objects and sensory experiences. Two of his major writings are *Leonard and Gertrude* (1781-81), and *How Gertrude Teaches Her Children* (1801).

A true humanist, Pestalozzi believed in education for social reform, and he promoted professional training for teachers.

Froebel

Friedrich Wilhelm August Froebel (1782-1852) is the German educator remembered most as the founder of the first kindergarten (1837). He also embraced Rousseau's view that man is inherently good. Froebel's view verged on pantheism as he spoke of a "spark of the divine" in each child. He romanticized childhood to the point of idolatry.

In Froebel's view the child's greatest need was for self-expression. The kindergarten was to be a place where the child can grow as freely as plants. He emphasized creating a pleasant environment where the child could learn by play. To Froebel play was the fulfillment of humanity. The teacher should cooperate with the play instincts of the child and be mainly a stimulator and encourager in the unfolding of the divinely endowed nature of the child. Froebel believed the child learned best through self-activity and group activities where he could learn to develop important habits of cooperation. It was the social experience that constituted the core of the true education for Froebel.

Froebel's teaching inaugurated a movement that has had immeasurable influence on modern education at all levels. The kindergarten movement meant education by the development of the potentialities of the holy child and is "something more fundamental than instruction in the Three R's."[24] The kindergarten movement held that:

> "Education is a process of development rather than a process of instruction; that play is the natural means of development during the early years; that the child's creative activity must be the main factor in his education; and that his present interests and needs rather than the demands of the future should determine the material and method to be employed,---all these principles underlying kindergarten procedure the psychologist approve, not for kindergarten alone but for all education."[25]

---

[24] Nina C. Vandewalker, *The Kindergarten in American Education* (New York: Macmillan, 1908), 1f.
[25] Ibid., 245.

America's first private kindergarten was established in 1856. The first public kindergarten was founded in 1873. In its early years kindergarten caused problems for the elementary teachers. Here is an account from a report written in 1899:

"First grade teachers confide to their superintendents that they would prefer children who have not attended the kindergarten to those who have. They fail to find any product in the kindergarten training of which the school can make use, and, on the other hand, they whisper that the kindergarten children are unruly, lack a spirit of obedience, are dependent, and continually expect to be amused."[26]

We no longer hear of kindergarten as a problem. This is because Froebel's thinking has prevailed. The kindergarten movement has won the philosophic battle. Today kindergarten is a fact of life in American public education, and Froebel's philosophy has extended way beyond the borders of the kindergarten classroom. His thinking dominates education in elementary schools and has had great influence on American education at all levels.

The Biblical Tradition in Education

The most significant event in history since the writing of the Bible to positively influence education is the Reformation.

The Reformation

Luther, Calvin, and virtually all the reformers placed a high premium on education, especially literacy. One of the cornerstones of the Reformation was the restoration of the Bible as the infallible Word of God and the supreme authority, replacing the Catholic concept of the supremacy of the Pope. It was now the responsibility of every individual Christian to know the Bible, but the common man in those days was usually illiterate. (It should be noted that in pagan societies literacy is usually restricted to the nobility, the government bureaucracy, and the religious hierarchy. In this sense, pre-Reformation Europe was more humanistic than biblical, more fruit of the laxity and corruption in the Church itself.)

Thus learning to read became a high priority. God providentially set the stage through Johan Gutenberg who invented the printing press in 1436, so that printing was fairly well developed by Luther's time. Translating the Bible into native languages also became a preoccupation of the reformers. True Biblical Christianity has done more to teach the world to read than any other influence in history. The Wycliffe Bible translators alone have been responsible for the development of literacy in hundreds of people groups around the world. More importantly, the philosophy of education based upon the biblical worldview promotes learning to read like no other philosophy.

The Puritans

It would be difficult to overstate the influence of the Puritans on American education. No other group settling in North America had the passion to establish literacy and sound education as the Puritans did. They brought the Reformation to America. Their religion was their first priority in life, and they intended to build a society in the New World based upon the Word of God. They, much more than Christians of our day, held a clear biblical worldview and

---

[26] Frederic Burk, *A Study of the Kindergarten Problem in the Public Kindergartens of Santa Barbara, California, for the year 1898-9* (San Francisco: Whitaker and Ray, 1899), 29.

understood its importance. Other groups settling in North America lacked the vision and passion for education held by the Puritans. As a result, the Puritan vision dominated. Some of the evidence of the Puritan influence on American education is given below.

Harvard

The Puritans were some of England's leading intellectuals. They saw no dichotomy between faith and reason, between accepting the authority of the Bible and intellectual pursuit. For the Puritans, scholarship and Christianity went hand in hand. Puritan pastors were among the most highly educated people in the local community. Establishing a college for the training of ministers was a natural priority for the Puritans. What is amazing is how quickly they acted to found Harvard. The great migration of Puritans to New England did not get underway until 1630. It took them a mere six years to establish Harvard in 1636 as the first college in America.

The Old Deluder Law

The Puritan understanding of the importance of literacy to a biblical worldview is illustrated in their passing of the Old Deluder Law in Massachusetts in 1647. The law provided that when a local community reached a population of fifty families, money should be raised to employ a teacher, and when a community reached a population of one hundred families, a grammar school should be built. The reason given for this law was to enable the population to read because of their great need to gain knowledge of the Bible. The law got its name from its preamble which stated, "It being the chief purpose of that old deluder, Satan, to keep men from the knowledge of the Scriptures. . ."[27]

The New England Primer

The New England Primer was the first textbook printed in America (1690). It became the main tool for teaching reading in the English colonies. During the late 1600's and early 1700's over three million were printed. This book taught the alphabet and reading by a phonetic use of syllables, but it was more than a reading primer. By using scripture passages, The Shorter Catechism, and stories and articles of a religious nature, the New England Primer was a major influence in inculcating the basic truths of Christianity to the population of New England.

Noah Webster

In 1783 the New England Primer was eclipsed by the famous "Blue-backed Speller" published by Noah Webster. Written in the tradition of the New England Primer, the Blue-backed Speller had even greater influence than its predecessor. Webster's speller sold over one hundred million copies in the eighteenth and nineteenth centuries. Like the Primer, the Blue-backed Speller had the double agenda of literacy and knowledge of the truth of Christianity, but it was more ambitious and scholarly in its purpose. It was part of Webster's larger work entitled, *A Grammatical Institute of the English Language*, which taught not only spelling, but also grammar and reading.

Although secular historians neglect him and dismiss him, Noah Webster has had a greater positive influence on American education than any other person in history. He was a committed Christian deeply devoted to Jesus Christ. At the same time, he was a genuine intellectual and a dedicated scholar. His biblical worldview is perhaps best expressed in his monumental work, *An American Dictionary of the English Language*, published in 1828. His

---

[27] Verna M. Hall, *The Christian History of the Constitution* (San Francisco: FACE, 1966), 273.

original dictionary defined words as the Bible used them and used scripture as illustrations of the use of words.

Literacy in Early America

English speaking colonial America had the highest literacy rate to date of any nation in history. The message of the American Revolution was spread by the printed word. Sermons were almost always written, printed, distributed, and widely read. During the debate over the adoption of the U.S. Constitution, arguments were promoted through the distribution of the famous Federalist Papers which were so scholarly that twentieth century university graduate students have much difficulty comprehending them, yet they were read and understood by the average New England farmer of that time.

The McGuffey Readers

Although secular influences grew stronger during the nineteenth century, the biblical worldview was still strong in America's schools. The McGuffey Readers were a major cornerstone to American education during the nineteenth century. Written as a reading textbook for several grade levels, the McGuffey readers sold over one hundred and twenty-two million copies in seventy-five years. The stories in the books promoted Christian principles intended to develop Christian character in America's children. The first readers were printed in 1836. Early editions contained much more reference to God and the Bible than later editions. By the twentieth century the religious content of the McGuffey readers had been greatly watered-down.

Biblical Jurisdiction of Education

<u>Goals:</u>

1. To gain a deeper understanding of the biblical concept of spheres of jurisdiction.
2. To increase awareness of the importance of following biblical principles that determine the roles of family, church, and state.

<u>Assignment:</u>

1. Read Lesson 4.
2. Write answers to Study Questions below.

<u>Study Questions:</u>

1. Explain how the Bible designates spheres of jurisdiction.
2. Why is following the biblical pattern of spheres of jurisdiction important?
3. How was Horace Mann a humanist?
4. What are the results of America's paradigm shift in the jurisdiction of education?
5. What is wrong with state certification of teachers?
6. What is the education industry and what are the dangers of having a large education industry?

<u>For Further Study (see resource list):</u>

Blumenfeld, Samuel L. *NEA: Trojan Horse in American Education.* Boise, ID: The Paradigm Company, 1984.

De Mar, Gary. *God and Government (Three Volumes).* Atlanta: American Vision, 1997.

Rushdoony, Rousas J. *The Messianic Character of American Education.* Vallecito, CA: Ross House Books, 1963.

Biblical Jurisdiction of Education

Although American education was firmly founded on a biblical worldview, today it is totally dominated by an anti-Christian humanistic worldview. America has undergone a tremendous paradigm shift in education. The term, paradigm, means model, blueprint, or the fundamental way we think about something. If we attempted to show graphically how American education has changed, it would look something like this.

The Great Paradigm Shift in American Education

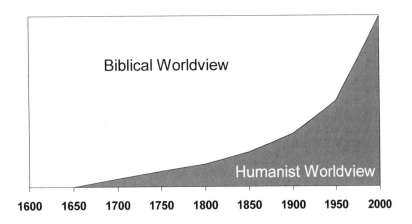

We started out right, but over the next four hundred years we Christians handed over control of American education to the humanists. In this section we will trace some of the milestones marking this transition. This paradigm shift can be studied in at least four aspects:

1. the jurisdiction of education
2. how we view human nature
3. the content of education
4. methods used in education.

The Great Paradigm Shift in Jurisdiction

The Bible clearly gives jurisdiction or responsibility for education to the family. In Ephesians 6:4 as in all other biblical passages concerned with the education of children, it is fathers who are charged with the responsibility; "*And, ye fathers, provoke not your children to wrath: but bring them up in the nurture and admonition of the Lord.*"

Scripture divides governmental responsibility into spheres of jurisdiction. In summary it looks like this:

Spheres of Government

The Family
- procreation of children
- rearing (education) of children
- provision for immediate and extended family

The Church
- proclamation of the gospel
- teaching and discipling of adults
- provision for those who have no family

The State
- administration of justice
- prohibit, prevent, prosecute, and punish injustice

Besides Ephesians 6, there are numerous passages in the Bible addressing parents, especially fathers, as the primary agent for the education of children. Throughout the book of Proverbs fathers are instructed on how to train their children. See also Deuteronomy chapter six.

Families are also charged with the responsibility for the provision and care of the immediate family. 1 Timothy 5:8 states: *"But if any provide not for his own, and especially for those of his own house, he hath denied the faith, and is worse than an infidel."* This responsibility also includes provision for extended family members. 1 Timothy 5:4 says: "But if any widow have children or nephews, let them learn first to show piety at home, and to requite their parents: for that is good and acceptable before God."

In Matthew 28: 19-20 the church is given responsibility to, *"Go ye therefore, and teach all nations, baptizing them in the name of the Father, and of the Son, and of the Holy Ghost: Teaching them to observe all things whatsoever I have commanded you: and, lo, I am with you alway, even unto the end of the world. Amen."*

Along with proclaiming the gospel, two other responsibilities are clearly given to the church. One is to provide for those who have no family. Particular attention is given to widows and orphans. See Acts 6:1-6, James 1:27, and Galatians 2:10. Note that the Bible does not promote the welfare state. Second Thessalonians 3:10 states: *"For even when we were with you, this we commanded you, that if any would not work, neither should he eat."* First Timothy 5: 3-10 underscores the biblical separation of spheres of governmental responsibility. Here it clarifies that the family, not the church, has responsibility for the provision and care of extended family members:

> *"Honour widows that are widows indeed. But if any widow have children or nephews, let them learn first to show piety at home, and to requite their parents: for that is good and acceptable before God. Now she that is a widow indeed, and desolate, trusteth in God, and continueth in*

supplications and prayers night and day. But she that liveth in pleasure is dead while she liveth. And these things give in charge, that they may   be blameless. But if any provide not for his own, and especially for those of his own house, he hath denied the faith, and is worse than an infidel. Let not a widow be taken into the number under threescore years old, having been the wife of one man, Well   reported of for good works; if she have brought up children, if she have lodged strangers, if she have washed the saints' feet, if she have relieved the afflicted, if she have diligently followed every good work."

As for the responsibility to teach, it is important to note that the Bible makes another important division of responsibility according to designated spheres of government. The commission to the church is to teach adults, not children. The passages in the Bible that command church leaders to teach refer to the teaching of adults. See Titus 2:1-3, 1 Timothy 4:11, 1 Timothy 3:2, and 2 Timothy 2:2. This of course has great implication to Christian educators.

The Bible is very clear that the primary responsibility for education of children belongs to the family. Thus the attitude that Christian parents can drop their children at the state's door to be educated by the civil government is in error. But so is the attitude that says Christian parents can drop their children at the church door and expect them to be educated by the church. The responsibility to bring up his children "in the nurture and admonition of the Lord" rests squarely on the shoulders of the father of the family.

Does this mean home schooling is the only legitimately biblical option? The answer lies in the understanding of jurisdiction. A father can send his child to a school outside his home without abdicating his jurisdiction, but this requires that he have a thorough knowledge of what kind of education his child will receive in that particular school. He needs to know if that school will assist him in bringing up his children in the "nurture and admonition of the Lord." Among other things, this school should educate children from a biblical worldview.

The purpose of this discussion is not to get the church off the hook, leaving the whole burden of education up to families. Higher education, meaning college and university, is not the education of children. Nor is high school education. High school age youth are not children. Despite how immature people are in their late teens today, they are not children. They would surely have been considered adults at the time the New Testament was written. It is the responsibility of the church to teach adults, young and old. The contemporary church has been very lax in obeying the Bible's commands to "teach," "instruct," and "disciple."

Furthermore, in its responsibility to teach adults, the church should be guiding parents in their biblical roles as parents. This includes guidance in educating their children. One of the great faults of the church today is its "hands off" attitude toward education. Pastors are just as guilty as parents in abdicating jurisdiction for education to the state.

As for civil government, the Bible clearly limits its jurisdiction to the administration of justice. Biblical scholars see Genesis 9:6 as God's establishment of civil government: *"And surely your blood of your lives will I require; at the hand of every beast will I require it, and at the hand of man; at the hand of every man's brother will I require the life of man. Whoso sheddeth man's blood, by man shall his blood be shed: for in the image of God made he man"* (Genesis 9:5-6). In this passage God is authorizing man to administer justice. *"Whoso sheddeth man's blood, by man shall his blood be shed."* Why does God do this? Because human life is precious in God's eyes, "for in the image of God made he man."

The scripture passage most commonly quoted describing civil government is Romans 13:1-7:

"Let every soul be subject unto the higher powers. For there is no power but of God: the powers that be are ordained of God. Whosoever therefore resisteth the power, resisteth the ordinance of God: and they that resist shall receive to themselves damnation. For rulers are not a terror to good works, but to the evil. Wilt thou then not be afraid of the power? Do that which is good, and thou shalt have praise of the same:

For he is the minister of God to thee for good. But if thou do that which is evil, be afraid; for he beareth not the sword in vain: for he is the minister of God, a revenger to execute wrath upon him that doeth evil. Wherefore ye must needs be subject, not only for wrath, but also for conscience sake. For this cause pay ye tribute also: for they are God's ministers, attending continually upon this very thing. Render therefore to all their dues: tribute to whom tribute is due; custom to whom custom; fear to whom fear; honour to whom honour."

All passages in the Bible that deal with civil government have to do with the administration of justice. Clearly the sphere of responsibility given to civil government is limited. Limited civil government is a biblical concept and it was one of the most important Christian concepts that our founders put into the American Constitution. Nowhere does the Bible authorize civil government to provide health care, retirement insurance, income for the unemployed, financial aid for all kinds of circumstances, and hundreds of other welfare services. Education certainly is not biblically within the sphere of civil government.

We live in a day when Christians have become lax in their reverence for the Word of God. We fail to appreciate the wisdom in the Bible that leads not only to eternal life, but to a better life on earth as well, a life that points to God and gives glory to Him. One of the areas in which we have become very lax is in this area of biblically defined spheres of government. Biblical lines of governmental jurisdiction have been ignored. When God's ways are neglected we reap bad fruit. When we violate Biblical principles, we set ourselves on a course for destruction. Biblical roles for fathers and mothers have been ignored, and the Christian family has become dysfunctional. The biblical roles for the church and the civil government have been mixed and confused. The church has abdicated much of its responsibility to educate adults and care for the needy. As a result, civil government has overrun its biblically defined sphere of jurisdiction resulting in government-controlled schools and a socialistic welfare state. In this next section we will examine how violating biblically defined jurisdiction has led to the decay of American education.

The Great Paradigm Shift in Jurisdiction

<u>the biblical view</u> ⟶ <u>the humanist view</u>

family/church control	state control
private	public
parental prerogative	compulsory laws
private funding	mandatory taxation

For the first two hundred years of America's history (1620-1820) American Christians maintained biblical jurisdiction over education. Virtually all children were home schooled or attended small local schools organized and funded by the local community. The Bible, Christian values, and the biblical worldview were integral to formal education at all levels. Secular education was virtually nonexistent. Textbooks were full of biblical indoctrination. The

Bible was used in every school. There were no state boards of education. Education was firmly under the control of the family and the church. It was private. Parents had the prerogative to educate their children at home or send their children to the school of their choosing. There was no state control of education, no mandatory taxation for the support of state schools, and no state laws compelling school attendance.

Over time Christians abdicated their responsibility to educate their children. The weakening of the church is often the result of a weakening in its theology. A very significant theological event took place in 1805. Author Sam Blumenfeld considers this the most important event in American history. That was the year that the control of the intellectual and theological center of American life, Harvard College, fell into the hands of those who espoused a Unitarian theology. Out of this grew a significant and widening difference in worldview between those Unitarians who controlled the intellectual establishment and what was at first the majority of orthodox pastors and their congregations. In time the whole church was affected. The growing liberalism of the nineteenth and twentieth century American church can be traced back to this date. One of the most significant figures in American history produced by this change was Horace Mann.

Horace Mann

Horace Mann (1796-1859) rejected his orthodox Christianity as a young man and embraced the growing intellectual trend of his day which was basically Unitarian. In those days Unitarianism was new and greatly mixed into many mainline Christian churches, especially in New England. A desire for creating a better society on earth with the use of Christian morals was often the preoccupation of this trend. The Bible, for example, was valued as a code of ethics, but Unitarianism and the new liberal view dismissed the inerrant authority of the Bible. This new man-centered approach also discouraged personal devotion to Jesus Christ and other forms of piety that humbled man and lifted up God.

Mann had strong Utopian tendencies. One of his heroes was Robert Owen who attempted to establish the socialistic community of New Harmony, Indiana in 1814. New Harmony boasted having America's first free public schools. The community failed. Mann was also enamored by the Prussian national school system. Prussia, a militaristic state, built its school system around the concept of training children to build a strong nation by filling its military and industrial workforce needs. Mann saw education as the means to build the better society. Although modern Americans would probably not be shocked by the thought of education as a means to build a better society, this concept is totally unbiblical, and many Christians of Mann's day knew it. To the early American Christian, education was a means to raise a child in the ways of the Lord and to prepare him to live a life useful for bringing glory to God, not the state.

Mann believed every human had "an absolute right" to an education and that it was the "duty of government" to provide it. One of Mann's most famous quotes sums up his naïve idealism:

"The common school is the greatest discovery ever made by man. Other social organizations are curative and remedial; this is a preventive and an antidote. Let the common school be expanded to its capabilities---- and nine-tenths of the crimes in the penal code would become obsolete, the long catalogue of human ills would be abridged; men would walk more safely by day; every pillow would be more inviolable by night; property, life, and character held by a stronger tenure; all rational hopes respecting the future brightened."[28]

Although he had very limited experience as an educator himself, Mann was a very active organizer and promoter. His efforts were major in the establishment of the first state controlled public schools in America. The first was 1818 in Boston. He pioneered the establishment of the first state board of education in Massachusetts (1837), he sponsored the first state compulsory education law, and he established the first state "normal" school to train teachers (Massachusetts 1838).

Most textbooks honor Mann as the "Father of Public Education." It would be more accurate to call him the "Father of Humanistic Education." Author, Marshall Foster sums up Mann's accomplishments from a more Christian perspective:

"In 1838 Horace Mann became the (first) Secretary of the Massachusetts Board of Education. Did you know that in the following years Mann promoted a philosophy of education that was diametrically opposed to that of the Founding Father generation? He is known as the father of the public school movement:

1. He supported forced taxation for state schools which undermined parental control and was detrimental to the private schools.
2. Mann, and those who followed him, de-emphasized the Biblical doctrine of salvation as the basis of character development, replacing it with the optimistic, humanistic view of the perfectibility of man through education and environment.
3. He encouraged group thinking and study rather than individual initiative and creativity.
4. He standardized teacher training, textbooks, and accreditation beginning the transition away from the principles of the Christian philosophy of education taught by the great founder of America's education system, Noah Webster."[29]

God is a God of order. Men would do well to learn God's ways, for violating God's principles has its consequences. Allowing the civil government to take control of education was the beginning of the corruption of American education. Many conservative Christian pastors of that time knew that violating biblical principles would bring problems, and they resisted Mann's movement. But over the course of the nineteenth century the liberals won out and state controlled public schools became the norm in American education.

The first public schools looked very much like the locally controlled community schools. They used the Bible, taught Christian values, and generally taught from a biblical worldview, but the seeds of destruction had been sown.

Some of the corollaries of this shift in the jurisdiction of education are listed in the following chart. We will discuss them in detail below.

---

[28] Horace Mann, quoted in Samuel L. Blumenfeld, *Is Public Education Necessary?* (Boise, ID: The Paradigm Co., 1981), 211.
[29] Marshall Foster and Mary Elaine Swanson, *The American Covenant* (Thousand Oaks, CA: The Mayflower Institute, 1981), 9.

The Great Paradigm Shift in Jurisdiction

the biblical view ———————————————————▶ the humanist view

local control
(economical)

centralized control
(extremely expensive)

"common sense"

"professionals"
state certification
NEA
education industry

Increased Expense

State control meant the gradual loss of local control. Centralized control is always more bureaucratic and economically inefficient. State control meant the beginning of the unending increases in spending on public education, first at the state level and later at the national level.

By 1905 twenty-two percent of all public expenditures went toward education. By mid-twentieth century the federal government began to get heavily involved in the financing (and, therefore, control) of education. In 1958 the federal government began major subsidizing of higher education in the form of student loans through the National Defense Education Act. The NDEA was a Cold War response to Soviet advances in science that put their first man in outer space. In 1965 the first version of the National Elementary and Secondary Education Act was passed by the U.S. Congress. This mammoth bill provides federal funding for numerous aspects of public education. The bill gets renewed every few years only to become more expensive and more encompassing. Much of what is "politically correct" in public schools is controlled by finances that come from the NESEA. By the end of the twentieth century the United States was the home of the most expensive education in the world. And even though we spent more than all other nations (it cost approximately $6,000 per year per pupil by the end of the century), we consistently score lower than most other developed nations in academic comparisons.

The Control of Teachers

Some Christian schools today require their teachers to have state teaching certificates. Most Americans think state certified teachers are a good thing. But if we believe the Bible does not approve of state control of education, we must reject state certification as unbiblical. Certification is control. Horace Mann knew certification was the way to control teachers. This is why he pushed for the establishment of state teacher colleges and state teacher certification.

It is especially hard to believe that Christians today would see state certification as positive when you consider all the anti-Christian requirements involved in getting certified. Most states require courses that promote multiculturalism, acceptance of homosexuality, and a host of other anti-biblical positions.

"But how do you insure competence?" one might ask. First of all, we should ask, "Whose concept of competence?" Currently state certified teachers are "competent" from a secular humanist point of view, but not from a biblical point of view. This is why we have certification by Christian school associations. If Christian school associations exist to support the family and the church in their legitimate control of education, this is the kind of certification Christians should want, not the opinion of the humanists.

State certification is unbiblical and has been a powerful tool in the humanist takeover of American education. In the 1830's Horace Mann pushed for state certification of teachers in Massachusetts. It was a new concept then. By the middle of the twentieth century it was the norm for the whole nation.

Teachers as "Professionals"

The term "professional" usually carries a favorable social stigma in our culture. Probably most Christian teachers would consider being called a professional as a positive thing. Again, whether it is positive or not depends on where you get your authority to be a professional.

Christian teachers serve God according to his Word. The basis of their professionalism (or whatever other term one might prefer) is in their knowledge and faithfulness to God's truth whether it is known through revelation or through the study of His creation. For the Christian teacher, "professional" status does not come from state certification, membership in the NEA or other teacher's union, or even his college degree in education.

One of the results of the establishment of state teacher certification and college degrees in "Education" has been the creation of the "professional" status of teachers. Previously teachers were expected to have a certain command of the subject matter to be taught in the classroom and a general aptitude to work well with children. Educational Psychology was unheard of. (The "science" of psychology did not come on the scene until the late nineteenth century. We will deal with this in more detail later.) For the first two hundred years of America's history, teachers controlled their classrooms by the use of what was considered common sense. Common sense simply meant the common view of human nature held by the majority of the people of the day. From the colonial period until well into the twentieth century this common-sense, for the most part biblical, understanding of human nature was the view of the vast majority of Americans.

As teacher training was taken over by the state and colleges began to confer degrees in "Education" the teaching profession became secularized. The stigma of a good teacher changed from that of being a godly man or woman to that of having "professional credentials" which included a degree in "Education" and state certification.

We will deal with the content of secular teacher training in more detail later. Our purpose here is to note how the paradigm shift in jurisdiction has even caused us to redefine what we mean by "teacher."

One of the results of this new professional consciousness of teachers was the forming of professional teacher associations which grew into powerful teacher unions. The first of these associations, The National Teachers Association, was founded in 1857. In 1870 it changed its name to the National Education Association (NEA). Since then the NEA has grown to the single most powerful labor union, special interest group, and lobbying power in the history of this nation. It was the political power of the NEA that caused President Jimmy Carter, fulfilling a campaign promise, to create a cabinet level department for the implementation of federal control of education in 1980. Most Americans accept a federal Department of Education as if it was a part of our national government since its founding. It is important to realize that America got along just fine without a national Department of Education for 360 years and that it has only been with us for a little over 20 years.

Furthermore, the NEA has been one of the most powerful political forces supporting abortion, homosexuality, radical feminism, radical environmentalism, and a host of other anti-biblical, humanistic political causes. For proof all one needs to do is read the resolutions passed at every annual NEA convention. The Bible says you will know them by their fruit.

More and more Christian educators are seeing secular teacher training as of minimal value at best and anti-biblical at worst. Very few Christian teachers form their Christian philosophy of education based upon their teaching degree. Sadly, this is even true for many teachers who obtained their degrees in Christian colleges. Most Christian teachers that have a well-developed biblical philosophy of education have developed their philosophy through knowledge of the Bible, books on education written from a biblical worldview, and on-the-job experience.

The Education Industry

Another result of this paradigm shift in the jurisdiction of education is the consolidation of power into a self-serving, all-controlling education industry. This is seen in the government bureaucracy itself. Today there are thousands of "education" employees that never go inside a classroom. They are the bureaucrats employed by the federal and state departments of education. Although there may be many well-meaning individuals employed in these jobs, when it comes to politics these groups consistently push for the continuation and expansion of government involvement in education. Job security is their priority number one.

Another component of the education industry is the education departments at colleges and universities. As more and more states made a degree in "Education" a requirement for teacher certification, colleges experienced an increase in enrollment that grew into healthy "Education Departments" and even "Schools of Education." Thus, another whole economic entity became dependent on government involvement in education.

We also have the textbook and education materials industry. Although Noah Webster's famous spelling books sold millions, they were not required by any government agency. Today many states, Texas for example, have agencies that determine what textbooks can and cannot be used in their public schools. Hundreds of textbooks are written to please these government agencies in order to get on state approved lists. Because of centralized control and huge sales agreements, smaller and often more innovative publishers are at a disadvantage.

Then there are the education "think tanks." These are research institutes and experimental schools that operate from money granted to them by government agencies and private institutions like the Carnegie Foundation. These projects, which provide lucrative careers for some of the most humanistic thinking authors and college professors, are guaranteed to be humanistic in their worldview by virtue of the "separation of church and state" myth that only allows money to flow to "non-religious" projects.

Probably the worst facet of this education industry is its narrow-mindedness. In spite of all the liberal talk about diversity, the education industry is intolerant of any views other than the secular humanist view. Vicious ostracizing is often the punishment given to anyone who suggests teaching methods that conflict with the views of the education industry. There is, for example, a strong bias against teaching methods associated with traditional education. This will be explained in detail when we discuss the paradigm shift in teaching methods.

As the graphic at the beginning of this section illustrates, this paradigm shift (as with each of the other aspects of paradigm shift we shall study) started out slow but the rate of change has been accelerating rapidly. For example, the role of the federal government in education is rather recent (the Department of Education was created in 1979 by president Jimmy Carter), but in that short time span the federal government's control has become a relentless vice that threatens to crush any form of real diversity in American education. The culmination of this movement was hatched in 1991, originally named "America 2000." Now, at the turn of the twenty-first century, renamed "Goals 2000," this all-encompassing plan for a singular national curriculum threatens totalitarian control over American education. Several other names have been used to continue the paradigm shift into a fully secular philosophy of education including, Race to the Top, No Child Left Behind and now Common Core.

Lesson 5

Content from the Biblical Worldview

Goals:

1. To gain a deeper understanding of how content is determined by the philosophy of education.
2. To increase awareness of the importance of knowing and appreciating our Christian heritage.
3. To gain a deeper understanding of how a nation's worldview affects the life of its people.

Assignment:

1. Read Lesson 5.
2. Write answers to Study Questions below.

Study Questions:

1. Content in humanistic education is "ideologically determined." What does that mean?
2. How has humanistic education devalued accuracy?
3. How are the goals of humanistic education different from traditional "liberal education"?
4. How are the humanistic view and the biblical view of history different? How will that affect content?
5. Why is regaining an appreciation for our Christian heritage important?
6. Explain how the biblical worldview is the reason for America's liberty and prosperity.
7. Explain why modern science developed in nations that held a biblical worldview rather than in nations that did not.
8. Why is it important to understand and teach the depravity of paganism?

For Further Study (see resource list):

Barton, David. "America's Godly Heritage" (video). Aledo, TX: WallBuilders, 1990.

Beliles, Mark A., and Stephen K McDowell. *America's Providential History.* Charlottesville, VA: Providence Foundation, 1989.

Hart, Benjamin. *Faith and Freedom.* Dallas: Lewis & Stanley, 1988.

Kennedy, D. James and Jerry Newcombe. *What if Jesus Had Never Been Born?* Nashville: Thomas Nelson, 1994.

Lesson 5

Content from the Biblical Worldview

The Great Paradigm Shift in Content

the biblical view		humanist view
abundant content	⟶	reduced content
"traditional" the three R's	⟶	ideologically determined multiculturalism sex education values clarification
accuracy important	⟶	devalued accuracy
"liberal education" "great books"	⟶	vocational training Goals 2000

The Decline of Content

In order to get into Harvard College in the seventeenth century a young boy (more often at fourteen to sixteen years old rather than at eighteen or nineteen as it is today) had to be able to read and write Latin and Greek.   Below is a partial reprint of a test eighth graders had to pass in order to enter high school in Indiana in the year 1910.

> High School Entrance Exam[30]
> State of Indiana---1911
> 1. In what state and on what waters are the following: Chicago, Duluth, Cleveland, and Buffalo? State an important fact about each.
> 2. What causes the change from day to night, and from summer to winter?
> 3. What is meant by inflection? What parts of speech are inflected?
> 4. Write a model business letter of not more than 40 words.
> 5. A rope 500 feet long is stretched from the top of a tower and reaches the ground 300 feet from the tower; how high is the tower?
> 6. Write a brief biography of *Evangeline*.
> 7. Give the structure of a muscle and the spinal cord.
> 8. Define arteries, veins, capillaries, and pulse.

It is highly probable that the majority of incoming college freshmen today would have trouble passing the high school entrance exam of 1911. Scores of books have been written over the last two decades that describe the "dumbing down" of American education. Evidence

---

[30] Gabler, Mel and Norma with James C. Hefley, *What Are They Teaching Our Children?* (Wheaton, IL: Victor Books, 1985), 20-21.

illustrating the watering down of content in textbooks is abundant. Many excuses have been presented defending this trend: "Children of the past were overwhelmed with irrelevant facts; Process is more important than content; Children should spend less time accumulating information and more time learning by experience," etc., but few would deny that the content of modern American education is quantitatively inferior to past generations.

As a matter of fact, knowledge itself has been devalued. We live in a culture that loves to express its opinions but has little patience with the process of gathering factual information. This is the age of the call-in talk show. Everybody loves to give his opinion. Facts have taken a back seat. From kindergarten on, teachers tend to be more concerned with a child's self-expression than with his learning of facts, let alone "truth."

This is part of the result of the great paradigm shift this nation has undergone regarding its view of knowledge, the content of education. This trend is altogether consistent with the humanist worldview. Humanism in its exaltation of man always emphasizes subjectivity over objectivity.

This was not the case in Noah Webster's day. From a biblical perspective, knowledge is very important. Knowledge is the substance of education. First, knowledge of God is important. Jesus compared the truth of the Word of God to bread, a vital necessity for life itself. Christianity is a religion based upon facts. Jesus became man at a specific time and place in history. His death and resurrection are historical facts. The apostle Paul said if Jesus' resurrection were not an historical fact, we would be fools to follow Christ. *"And if Christ be not risen, then is our preaching vain, and your faith is also vain"* (1 Corinthians 15:14).

According to Bloom's famous taxonomy of higher and lower order thinking skills[31], absorbing information is the lowest of the lower order thinking skills. A summary of his ranking looks like this:

Bloom's Taxonomy

	Evaluation
Higher Order	Synthesis
	Analysis
- - - - - - - - - -	
	Application
Lower Order	Comprehension
	Information

Many educators today feel an urgency to move students into analysis, synthesis, and evaluation. Children at a very young age are asked to make evaluations and form opinions based on very little knowledge of the subject at hand. Children are urged to express "how they

---

[31] Robert F. Biehler and Jack Snowman, *Psychology Applied to Teaching: Seventh Edition* (Boston: Houghton Mifflin, 1993), 279-281. Note that information on Bloom's Taxonomy is available in practically all college textbooks on education.

feel about" the subject being discussed. Discussions and debates are preferred over reading and research. This approach might make a class more "fun," but it puts the emphasis in the wrong place and shortchanges children in their learning of content.

When the emphasis is all on the "higher order" thinking skills a very important aspect is overlooked. The "higher order" skills depend upon prior acquisition of the "lower order" thinking skills. We can't comprehend until we acquire information. We can't make application until we comprehend, and we certainly can't make evaluations without information (knowledge).

Politically Correct Content

When America was dominated by the biblical worldview, the content or "subject matter" in our schools was commonly referred to as the "three R's" of reading, writing, and arithmetic. What we commonly refer to as "traditional education" included these basic skills along with the study of history, geography, and science. Government control of education has opened the door for all kinds of special interest groups to inject their particular views into the public-school curriculum. Rather than being determined by the common sense of what a child needs to learn, today's curriculum is ideologically determined. Precious hours of the school day are spent on drug awareness, sex education, multiculturalism, values clarification, "diversity" or life-style tolerance, and even death education. Even the traditional subjects have been saturated with the politically correct humanistic worldview. History books have been revised to the point they have become propaganda tools for the radical feminist movement and other humanist political forces.

The Devaluation of Accuracy

Have you ever been frustrated waiting for the teenager behind the counter at the local fast food restaurant while he tries to make correct change? Have you noticed how nobody under 40 seems to know how to spell? Can you read anyone's handwriting unless they are over 60 years old? What is worse is that nobody seems to care. Accuracy just isn't important anymore. It is a growing national attitude. It starts in schools where spelling and grammar are not considered important. Children are not trained in accuracy because correction might inhibit their self-expression.

The dictionary defines accuracy as precision, exactness and conformity to fact. This lack of accuracy and attention to detail is beginning to have a serious detrimental effect on our nation. Students from the United States continue to score below the majority of the developed nations of the world in math and science. American graduate schools in science, math, engineering, and other high technology fields are filling up with foreign students because American students can't make the grade. Employers are frustrated with young employees who have this attitude that accuracy is not important. This was not a problem before this paradigm shift in the content of American schools.

This negative attitude toward accuracy has even affected Christian theology. Francis Schaeffer points out that even the word, "God," has lost its content. The modern notion of God, even in evangelical churches, has become subjective, experiential, and emotional rather than scripturally accurate.

From Liberal Education to Vocational Training

It is highly ironical that the employers of this nation are unhappy with the level of competency of the graduates of America's schools. Humanistic influences have been working to change the basic orientation of American education from what we usually call "liberal" education to a system of education whose main purpose is to fulfill the work needs of the national economy. A "liberal" education meant an education that liberated or set a person free. (Not to be confused with the term politically "liberal" or "left wing" politics.) The idea is compatible with the biblical concept that says, *"And ye shall know the truth, and the truth shall make you free"* (John 8:32). The goal of a liberal education was to produce a better person regardless of what career path he chose. The liberally educated man was to be a well-read, well-disciplined, artistically astute individual who had studied the ideas of the great thinkers of history. One of the most significant aspects of the paradigm shift in American education is this fundamental shift in the purpose of education.

Goals 2000 is a master plan for vocational training, not liberal education. Its agenda includes identification of a child's vocational interests and aptitudes at an early age and placing him on a track designed to prepare him for a specific career. In many states this process is called "Profiles in Learning." The agenda of making our schools vocational training centers is revealed in Goals 2000's other main component, the "School to Work" program.

This fundamental change in the purpose of education has a profound effect upon the content of the curriculum. In the past it was important to study the "great books" or the "classics." This generic term meant the writings of the great thinkers of history. It also meant a thorough knowledge of history itself. The curriculum of traditional education was much more content rich than modern humanistic education.

Reinstating Knowledge

We must recognize this state of knowledge anemia in American education. We live in an environment that has neglected substantial content in teaching and learning for several generations. Our degrees in education do not provide adequate background in subject matter for the traditional core curriculum. For the most part, a degree in education is basically indoctrination in humanistic psychology. (We will deal with this in more detail in a later section.) As educators we must start with an honest appraisal of our own lack of content knowledge. Discredited as it may be by modern humanistic educators, imparting knowledge is a major part of teaching. Is this not essentially what Jesus did? Noah Webster's 1828 dictionary defines impart as, "to give, grant or communicate; to bestow on another a share or portion of something." The bottom line is we can't impart something unless we first have it ourselves.

We must begin with our own acquisition of knowledge. Some Christian schools prefer that their teachers have degrees in a core subject like history or math rather than a degree in education. Where returning to college is impractical or unwise, we need to resort to self-education. Reading is essential, especially reading in history.

Teachers need a foundational knowledge of honest, accurate history. Those of us who do not know the truth about history are at the mercy of the anti-Christian revisionist historians. Christianity is an historical religion. Most of the Bible, both the Old Testament and the New Testament, is history. Contrary to the humanistic theories, history is not an account of random accidental incidents. It is not the record of the conflict of economic interests. It is not the glorious story of the evolution of man on to higher and better stages of humanity. From the biblical point of view history is the record of a sovereign God fulfilling His purposes in time. All true history gives glory to God. Christian teachers who gain a better understanding of history not only become better teachers, they experience a strengthening of their personal faith in God.

One of the problems, of course, is finding true history. Part of the worldview war has been the effort to discredit Christianity and God's name by revising the history books.

Fortunately, in recent years a number of grassroots Christian ministries have published history books written from a biblical worldview. See the resource list for the names of these organizations.

There was a time in America's past when history books were more reliable. Books written before 1900 tend to be more accurate and much more appreciative of Christianity's influence upon history.

Regaining Appreciation of Our Christian Heritage

One of the greatest tragedies of modern Christian education is its loss of appreciation for our Christian heritage. There is no doubt that we live in a cultural environment that is hostile towards Christianity, but the sad fact is that Christians themselves lack an appreciation of Christianity's positive influence upon history.

For example, when the author of this course was a young history teacher discussing the settling of the Western Hemisphere, he would often be asked, "Why did North America become so prosperous while South America remained undeveloped?" He would answer that North America's prosperity was due to its superior supply of natural resources. This answer comes from an economic interpretation of history based upon a naturalistic worldview, and it is blatantly wrong. South America is very rich in natural resources. The prosperity of the United States is a result of the biblical worldview of its settlers. An opportunity to restore appreciation for our Christian heritage was missed and the humanistic worldview was reinforced.

Many humanist historians portray Christianity as the cause of more harm than good. Nothing could be farther from the truth. The history of the human race was going downhill until Jesus Christ came to earth. There is no influence more positive in all of history than the influence of Christianity. Every part of the world that has been visited by Christianity has been better off for it. Where the biblical worldview is embraced, man is blessed.

This can be illustrated graphically by the following chart:

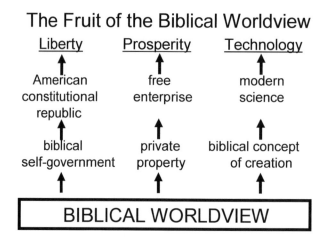

Blessings follow those who are faithful to God's Word. Nations that build their culture upon the biblical worldview experience more liberty, prosperity, and general high standard of living than nations that do not follow the biblical worldview. One might protest, "What about Western Europe? They have abandoned Christianity." Or they can even make a strong case that America is no longer a Christian nation. The answer lies in the fact that even though nations may be in the process of turning away from God, they still owe their liberty, prosperity, and technology to their Christian heritage. They will experience a loss of these blessings if they continue to turn away from God, but the blessings themselves can be attributed to no other source than their Christian heritage. The foundation of these blessings is the biblical worldview.

No one can honestly dispute that Americans enjoy a greater degree of liberty than any other people in history. We owe this to our Founding Fathers who established the American constitutional republic which was the best expression of a government built upon the biblical worldview to date in the history of the world. In spite of all the efforts of humanist historians, it cannot be denied that the biblical concept of self-government is what distinguishes the American republic. Likewise, we owe our prosperity to our free enterprise system which is based upon the biblical concept of private property, a fundamental aspect of the biblical worldview. Even the technology that makes our lives so convenient and comfortable owes its existence to the biblical worldview. Modern technology could not happen without modern science. No other worldview except the biblical worldview with its unique concept of creation was able to give birth to modern science.

Our chart is a sketchy explanation indeed. A thorough understanding of the cause-to-effect relationship of the biblical worldview to each of these blessings requires much more discussion than time allows here. Yet this is the kind of understanding that is so sorely needed by Christian educators. All we can do here is make the plea that they read, read, read.

Let us consider the blessing of modern science as an example of how the biblical worldview is the cause of blessing. It is no accident that modern science did not rise out of the cultural environment of Hinduism, Buddhism, or Islam. Modern science has distinctly Christian roots.

Worldview and the Rise of Science

Non-Biblical Worldviews	Biblical Worldview
Fear, Ignorance fear of nature (animism, pantheism)	Confidence, Knowledge transcendent creator orderly universe laws can be known
No Motivation fatalism (Hinduism, Buddhism, Islam)	Positive Motivation dominion mandate progress
Lack of Liberty pagan concept of government tyranny closed society	Liberty biblical concept of government freedom of thought experimentation, discovery

The pagan view of nature saw creation as inhabited by all kinds of spirits. Unexplainable phenomena were attributed to be the activity of various spirits that needed to be appeased. Nature was feared and worshipped. On the other hand, the biblical worldview explains that the universe was made by a transcendent Creator who is not part of nature but separate from and above nature. This Creator is a God of law and order. The universe is the result of an intelligent design. Man is created in the image of God with the ability to know certain laws of nature. Furthermore, the biblical worldview says that man was commanded to take dominion over the earth. He was not to fear nature; he was to exert a certain amount of control over it.

The other major religions of the world are plagued with fatalism. Hinduism sees nature as unending reoccurring cycles of which man has no control. Buddhism sees the material world as an illusion. Even Islam fails to provide motivation for man to study nature in order to take dominion over it.

Progress itself is a uniquely Christian concept. A missionary friend of the author related a story to illustrate this point. He was preaching in a non-Christian, undeveloped nation through an interpreter. At one point in his sermon the interpreter took an exceptionally long time to translate the missionary's English. This was followed by laughter from the audience at a point where the missionary had injected no humor. After the sermon the missionary asked the interpreter what happened.

"Well," said the interpreter, "at that point in your sermon you said, 'there must be a better way', so I said to the audience that you were a typical American, and they all laughed." It then occurred to the missionary that these people associated the concept of "a better way," or progress, with Americans. Up until that point he never realized that the concept of progress was foreign to their culture. As a matter of fact, the concept of progress is foreign to most cultures, but it is not uniquely American. It is uniquely Christian. It is the result of God's dominion mandate given to Adam to make the garden a better place.

The development of modern science requires liberty. The ability to make new discoveries requires an environment of freedom of thought that is not found in societies controlled by the pagan concept of government. Second Corinthians 3:17 states, *where the Spirit of the Lord is, there is liberty.* The converse is equally true. Where the Spirit of the Lord is not, there is tyranny. Essentially there are only two concepts of government, the biblical concept and the pagan or humanist concept. History verifies this fact. All non-biblical governments are man centered. Their highest authority is man. Since man is prone to evil because of the fall, non-biblical forms of government always end in tyranny. Only governments submitted to the higher law of God can provide liberty. (Note that the biblical concept of government is a very important aspect of developing one's biblical worldview. The subject deserves much more attention than the scope of this course allows. Please refer to the reference section for books on this subject.) The important point here is that the great emergence of modern science took place in the Western European and North American cultures where governments had been most influenced by the biblical worldview.

The Depravity of Paganism

A corollary to the appreciation of our Christian heritage is the appreciation of the depravity of paganism. The humanistic multicultural agenda tries to tell us that all cultures are of equal value. What they really are saying is that all religions are of equal value because religion is the chief factor in the formation of any culture. The religion provides the worldview and the worldview shapes the culture. One of the results of the humanist multicultural agenda is that it is now politically incorrect to say anything negative about primitive or "pagan" cultures. As a matter of fact, even the word "pagan" is politically incorrect. The intended result of this campaign is to put Christianity and paganism on the same level. This is revisionist history at its worst.

We need to teach truthfully about paganism. For most Christian teachers this probably means they must first learn the truth about paganism. Much myth has been promoted about primitive man. It began during the Romantic period of the Enlightenment with the writings of men like Rousseau who put forth the idea of the "noble savage." This naïve, uninformed image of uncivilized man is presented in practically all modern textbooks. The American Indians, or Native Americans to be politically correct, are presented as the ideal example of how man should interact with his natural environment. Small children are enamored with the idyllic lifestyle of the simple peace-loving Native Americans as they are presented in the modern multicultural classroom. We are warned not to impose "white man's values" on other cultures. George Washington was extremely politically incorrect in 1779 when he told the chiefs of the Delaware Indians that, "You do well to wish to learn our arts and our ways of life, and above all, the religion of Jesus Christ. These will make you a greater and happier people than you are; Congress will do everything they can to assist you in this wise intention."[32]

The truth is that pagan cultures are not a pretty sight. The Aztecs of Mexico, for example, slaughtered hundreds of thousands of their neighbors in human sacrifice to their pagan gods. Very little truth is mentioned in modern textbooks about the inferior status of women in the Native American or any other primitive culture. Nor do we get information about the infanticide, slavery, Stone Age living conditions, or the health and life expectancy of the people of these primitive cultures.

The same is true of modern textbook presentations of ancient Greek and Roman culture. Humanists of all eras have tended to idolize ancient Greece as the birthplace of all that is good in modern culture. The fact that "democracy" was only enjoyed by a small minority of the population, that a huge portion of the population was slave, that homosexual relations were valued more than women, and that abortion and infanticide were common practices all get overlooked.

It matters not what race or ethnic group a people belongs to. All cultures were depraved before Christianity visited their land. This includes pre-Christian Germany, England, Sweden, and every land on earth. Christian educators need to regain not only an appreciation of our Christian heritage, we need to learn and teach the truth about the depravity of pagan cultures. The multiculturalism agenda clouds the fact that all people groups need Jesus Christ.

---

[32] George Washington, *The writings of George Washington,* John c. Fitzpatrick, ed. (Washington, D.C.: U.S. Government Printing Office, 1932), Vol. XV, p. 55

Lesson 6

The Biblical View of Human Behavior

Goals:

1. To gain a deeper understanding of how modern psychology conflicts with the Bible.
2. To gain a deeper appreciation for the Bible as a guide to understanding human behavior.

Assignment:

1. Read Lesson 6.
2. Write answers to Study Questions below.

Study Questions:

1. Why is the Bible the greatest "psychology" book ever written?
2. Why is modern psychology unscientific?
3. How did Freud replace repentance with therapy?
4. How does the self-esteem movement conflict with the Bible?
5. How does Piaget's theory of moral development conflict with the Bible?

For Further Study (see resource list):

Kilpatrick, William. *The Emperor's New Clothes.* Ridgefield, CT: McCaffrey Publishing: 1985.

Noebel, David A. *Understanding the Times.* Manitou Springs, CO: Summit Press, 1991.

Lesson 6

The Biblical View of Human Behavior

Foundational to forming a philosophy of education is our understanding of human nature. If we want to think biblically in this area, we must start by examining the assumptions we hold about human behavior.

To whom do you turn for your understanding of human behavior?

• Freud		• Moses
• Skinner		• David
• Piaget	OR	• Solomon
• Rogers		• Luke
• Dewey		• Paul

The men on the left are the priests of a secular religion called modern psychology. On the right are the human writers of the inspired Word of God. The content produced by the men on the left is called the "science" of psychology which is scarcely over a hundred years old. The men on the right recorded the Creator's own description of human nature. We have had their writings for over two thousand years. Where do you turn for your understanding of human behavior?

Many Christians naively believe that these two sources are in agreement. This might be more the case if psychology were truly a "science." Unfortunately, modern psychology is much more theory based upon humanistic assumptions than it is true science. **The basic teachings of every one of the men listed on the left are in conflict with the Bible.** The parameters of this course only allow time to touch on a few of these theories, but an honest comparison of the theories of modern psychology with the Bible will reveal great contrasts in the understanding of human behavior. Several good books on this subject have come out in recent years. Please refer to the course resource list.

It is very possible that more humanistic thinking has crept into the Church through psychology than in any other way. The naïve faith in psychology is frequently expressed by Christians, including pastors, who recommend that Christians with marital problems seek "professional help," meaning secular counselors or psychologists. Even "Christian counseling" is often dominated by the unbiblical theories of modern psychology.

The unbiblical thinking of modern psychology has tremendous influence on the parenting practices of Christian parents. This reality can cause problems for a Christian school that is attempting to go against the cultural trends by applying biblical principles of discipline in the classroom.

Since virtually all teacher training textbooks, including those used in Christian colleges, are based upon modern psychology, anyone who gets a degree in education today has had their mind saturated with secular assumptions about human behavior. Christian educators must be willing to let go of these assumptions and allow the Word of God to govern their thinking about human behavior. We must come to appreciate the fact that the Bible is the best "psychology" book ever written. For two thousand years Christians successfully raised their children, solved their marital problems, and provided their children good education without modern psychology. It is no accident that as our culture abandoned biblical principles and embraced modern psychology, we saw an increase in divorce, mental illness, suicide, and many other "social" and "emotional" problems.

The following chart attempts to summarize some of the major changes that came from this great paradigm shift in America's understanding of human behavior.

The Great Paradigm Shift in Understanding Human Behavior

The Biblical View   The Humanist View

biblical understanding   ———————————▶   modern psychology

personal responsibility   ———————————▶   psychoanalysis

self denial   ———————————▶   self-esteem

traditional discipline   ———————————▶   permissivism

The term, psychology, comes from the Greek words psyche (soul) and logos (word). It originally meant the study of the soul or mind. Psychology's very definition creates a problem. Science is the study of the material world. To say that human behavior can be understood through the scientific method implies that human behavior is wholly understandable in terms of the physical world. This view denies the spirituality of man.

Behaviorism

The first books on modern psychology were written near the end of the nineteenth century during a time of great optimism about the potential of modern science. There was a growing belief that man's behavior could now be understood "scientifically," and the new "science" of psychology became an infatuation of the humanistic mindset. Evolution was gaining acceptance in the academic realm thanks to the tremendous influence of Darwin, and the first trends in modern psychology were to study human behavior from the assumption that man is an animal. The general term encompassing this trend is behaviorism.

Behaviorism ignores the spirituality of man. In fact, it denies any spiritual causality in human behavior. All behavior is defined in terms of physical response to external stimuli. The environment is the determiner of behavior. Man, rather than being an agent of spiritual influence upon the world, is a product of the environment. Behaviorism does not recognize the mind as a spiritual component, but rather sees the brain as a complex nervous system that merely responds to stimuli. The logical conclusion of behaviorism compels the denial of free will in human beings. B.F. Skinner (1904-1990), the great exponent of behaviorism, stated, "The hypotheses that man is not free is essential to the application of scientific method to human behavior."[33]

Behaviorism tempts men to think they can control society through behavior modification. The famous Russian psychologist, Ivan Pavlov (1849-1936) once said, "Only science, exact science about human nature itself, and the most sincere approach to it by the aid

---

[33] B.F. Skinner quoted by David A. Noebel, *Understanding the Times* (Manitou Springs, CO: Summit Press, 1991), 381.

63

of the omnipotent scientific method, will deliver man from his present gloom, and will purge him from his contemporary shame in the sphere of interhuman relations."[34] The desire to control men through social engineering is based upon a faith in behaviorism. This same mentality brought about the birth of the "social sciences" of sociology and political "science." It spawned the endless train of "scientific studies" of human behavior funded at taxpayers' expense. This kind of thinking applied to education has led to America's current all-encompassing education project, Goals 2000. Goals 2000, the epitome of social engineering, is nothing less than an attempt to control the whole population of a nation through behavior modification.

The teaching method based upon the assumptions of behaviorism is behavior modification. This will be discussed in the section on teaching methods.

Freud

The second great influence in the rise of modern psychology was Sigmund Freud (1856-1939). Freud saw all human motivation as coming from basic instinctive animal drives found deep inside all human beings. He constructed a theory of human behavior based entirely upon these carnal instincts. He proposed that human behavior could be understood by uncovering these drives found deep in a person's subconscious. In the subconscious Freud found all kinds of nasty human motivation. In the sense that the human heart is full of wickedness, Freud's theory was closer to Christian belief on this point than many other psychologists. The Bible says, *"The heart is deceitful above all things, and desperately wicked: who can know it?"* (Jeremiah 17:9) Freud's error (among many errors) was that he did not accept the reality that man is a spiritual being, that his heart is spiritual, and that his heart is corrupted because of man's sin.

This difference of view has enormous consequences. According to Freud the root cause of man's behavior is carnal. Therefore, the remedy for bad behavior is therapy. According to the Bible there is only one remedy for bad behavior. That remedy is repentance.

It is nearly impossible to overestimate Freud's influence on modern America's thinking about human behavior. Even though there are numerous books criticizing Freud for his lack of scientific objectivity (which is powerful evidence that modern psychology is not scientific), his ideas have captured American culture.

His influence changed the way Americans interpret human behavior. Before Freud, a man's behavior was judged by moral standards found in the Bible. If a man intentionally took the life of another, he was judged guilty of murder. Subconscious motivation was not a factor.

Since Freud, we have become preoccupied with people's subconscious motives. Practically all behavior today is subject to psychological analysis. Amateur psychoanalysis by every Tom, Dick, and Harry has replaced baseball as America's favorite pastime.

Freud's theories conflict with the Bible on numerous points. Perhaps the most significant is in the area of personal responsibility. When America accepted the biblical understanding of human behavior, men were held responsible for their behavior. Thanks to Freud, it is now possible to be excused from almost any behavior, including criminal behavior. Judges excuse criminals and parents excuse their children's wrong behavior because of Freudian thinking that makes the emotional state of the perpetrator more important than his actions. We can thank Freud and his successors for the trend toward permissivism in American parenting and teaching.

---

[34] Ivan P. Pavlov quoted by David A. Noebel, *Understanding the Times* (Manitou Springs, CO: Summit Press, 1991), 377.

The Self-esteem Movement

In the 1950's and 1960's a "third force" in psychology came on the American scene. Based upon the writings of Carl Rogers and Abraham Maslow, this school of psychology emphasized self-esteem. Maslow believed that humans could only become contributors to society after their own needs had been met. He created an elaborate hierarchy of needs of which self-esteem was essential. In essence he threw out the traditional view of self-respect which said a person gained a sense of satisfaction about themselves as a result of accomplishment. In its stead his self-esteem philosophy maintained that a good feeling about oneself must precede accomplishment.

It is amazing how many Christians have bought into the self-esteem movement when it is clearly in conflict with the Bible's message of self-denial. Even Christian educators have swallowed the myth that the first goal of education is that a child feel good about himself. Scripture has been reinterpreted from a self-esteem movement perspective. "Love thy neighbor as thyself" has been twisted to proclaim that, "you can't love your neighbor until you first love yourself." The self-esteem movement is exactly the kind of philosophy based upon the principles of this world that Paul warned about in Colossians 2:8, and unfortunately, it is a prime example of how Christians can be taken captive by unbiblical thinking.

The Bible preaches self-denial. Self-denial is the practice of obeying God's will while trusting Him to meet one's needs. It is acting in faith. Maslow's theory says a person must have the need of feeling good about himself met first. The Bible says, *"But seek ye first the kingdom of God, and his righteousness; and all these things shall be added unto you."* (Matthew 6:33). The commensurate passage on this issue is Matthew 16:24-25. *"Then said Jesus unto his disciples, If any man will come after me, let him deny himself, and take up his cross, and follow me. For whosoever will save his life shall lose it: and whosoever will lose his life for my sake shall find it."* Self-denial is an essential character quality of a mature Christian.

Piaget

The psychology that has perhaps had the greatest influence on the education of children was that of Jean Piaget (1896-1980). Piaget was a Swiss psychologist known for his theory of cognitive and intellectual development. His thinking dominates modern child psychology. He may not always be acknowledged as the source, but his theories are the foundation for most of the material in child psychology and educational psychology books written today. Piaget dedicated his life to the study of children's behavior and is highly regarded among psychologists. It is almost sacrilegious to criticize his contribution yet criticize it we must. As believers in the Bible, we must reject Piaget's major theory, the moral development of the child.

Piaget believed the moral development of a child was a process of natural maturation. He identified what he called stages of moral development. Each stage is characterized by the person's primary motive for moral behavior. In stage one, the obedience and punishment stage, a small child's main motivation for his behavior is said to be avoidance of punishment. According to the theory, in stage two, the "back scratching" stage, a child learns the value of doing something in expectation of getting a return favor ("You scratch my back, and I'll scratch yours.") Conformity to the group is supposed to be the main motivation for stage three. By stage four, the desire for law and order is said to be the prime motive. In stage five the individual is supposed to have arrived at a higher understanding and appreciation of moral guidance that comes from society. This "social contract" stage is only surpassed by the highest level of moral development according to Piaget, stage six. In stage six an individual bases his moral decisions on an understanding and appreciation of universal principles which are discoverable by human reason. Does this sound more like philosophy than science? It should, because it is. Even Piaget considered himself first a philosopher and secondly a psychologist.

The main conflict between Piaget and the Bible has to do with how we as parents and teachers should cultivate moral development in a child. Piaget believed moral development was a natural process that every human being should go through without intervention from adults. Having been a Professor at the Jean Jacques Rousseau Institute in Paris, it should not be a surprise that Piaget subscribed to the Rousseau's Enlightenment philosophy of the basic goodness of human nature. According to Piaget, correction, and especially physical chastisement like spanking, is very harmful to a child's development. Piaget opposed any form of moral indoctrination.

This of course flies in the face of both the American Christian tradition and the Bible's instructions to parents. The New England Primer, Noah Webster's Blue Backed Speller, and even the McGuffey Readers were all forms of moral indoctrination. The Bible is full of admonishments to parents to train, teach, instruct, and correct their children. The biblical view of humanity is clear. Man has a fallen nature and cannot save himself. He is desperately in need for truth that comes from outside his self. According to the Bible, moral instruction is needed and parents are commanded to give it to their children.

Unfortunately Piaget's view, not the Bible's, has come to dominate thinking about child development. According to modern psychology, child rearing and educational practices based upon the Bible are harmful to a child's mental health. Dr. Chester Pierce, Professor of Education and Psychiatry at Harvard University said in 1972, "Every child in America entering school at the age of five is insane because he comes to school with certain allegiances toward our founding fathers, toward his parents, toward a belief in a supernatural being, toward the sovereignty of this nation as a separate entity. It's up to you teachers to make all of these sick children well by creating the international children of the future."[35]

One of the major developments in education based upon Piaget's thinking is the concept of "values clarification." Sidney Simon is known as one of the main proponents of the concept of "values clarification" which is widely used under a variety of names in America's schools today. His thinking is the basis for the predominant philosophy used in drug abuse education. It is based on the assumption that children will reason to avoid drug abuse by exploring its probable consequences. Like most other humanist psychologists, Simon agrees with Piaget regarding the moral development of a child. In 1966 he wrote in the book, *Values and Teaching*,

"There is the idea that the child needs to be really free to choose. . . Moralizing has not worked in the past; do not be afraid to abandon it as a classroom practice. . . We are primarily concerned with the process that a person uses to get at a value, not with what value he chooses at any one time and place---we are concerned with the process of valuing and not particularly with the product."[36]

Simon is wrong. Moralizing does work. The statistics are there for everyone to see. When moral indoctrination was a main part of American education we had far less drug abuse, sexual promiscuity, divorce, abortion, suicide, etc. than we have since the humanistic "hands off" approach was embraced. Replacing Biblical principles with modern psychological theories

---

[35] Chester A. Pierce, quoted in James R. Patrick, *Research Manual: America 2000/Goals2000* (Moline IL: Citizens for Academic Excellence, 1994), 86.

[36] Sidney Simon, quoted in James R. Patrick, *Research Manual: America 2000/Goals2000* (Moline IL: Citizens for Academic Excellence, 1994), 76.

has contributed tremendously to the destruction of America. Our concern here is that Christian educators recognize its harmful influence, that they examine their own assumptions and practices, and be willing to let go of humanistic thinking and turn to the Bible for guidance.

Lesson 7

Biblical Teaching Methods: Part I

<u>**Goals:**</u>

1. To gain a deeper understanding of why all teaching methods are not equal.
2. To gain a deeper appreciation of the importance of being principled.

<u>**Assignment:**</u>

1. Read Lesson 7.
2. Write answers to Study Questions below.

<u>**Study Questions:**</u>

1. How is the "dumbing down of America" a spiritual issue?
2. How was John Dewey a humanist?
3. What is the difference between being pragmatic and being principled?
4. Describe the anti-traditional education bias. Why is this significant?
5. What is the fundamental error of behavior modification? Why is behavior modification degrading to its subjects?

<u>**For Further Study (see resource list):**</u>

Rushdoony, Rousas J. *The Philosophy of the Christian Curriculum.* Vallecito, CA: Ross House Books, 1985.

Lesson 7

<u>Biblical Teaching Methods: Part I</u>

There is a common misconception among Christian educators that when we consider teaching the biblical worldview we are concerned about content only. It is widely held that teaching methods are neutral or that all methods are equal. This is why elementary grade teachers often take the attitude that the biblical worldview issue is a problem for the high school teachers. They reason that developing a worldview is a relatively mature intellectual process that happens in high school when students are able to deal with larger doses of abstract content like the study of the principles of American government or principles of economics. While it is true that high school students can deal with more abstract content, it is a mistake to think that worldview formation does not start until high school. It is also a mistake to think that teaching methods are neutral. The methods we use in the classroom from the very earliest grades have tremendous impact on a child's formation of his worldview.

All teaching methods are not equal. Every teaching method is based upon someone's educational philosophy, whether the teacher using the method is aware of it or not. Included in every educational philosophy are two elements that will determine the methods used by that philosophy. These are the philosophy's concept of truth and its concept of the nature of man. For example, if the philosophy views man as merely a highly evolved animal it will favor methods of behavior modification. If the philosophy sees man as created in the image of God with a spiritual mind, it will choose methods that impart truth.

The teaching methods a child is subjected to during his early years in school will have a great impact on the formation of his worldview. Some methods will cause a child to become passive and dependent. Others will inspire and encourage sound reasoning skills. Nothing more clearly illustrates this fact than the great "dumbing down" of America that we have experienced in the second half of the twentieth century. Numerous books have been written on this subject. However, very few of the experts understand that this "dumbing down" is at its core a spiritual issue.

The logic goes like this. As a nation we gradually rejected a philosophy of education based upon biblical principles. We substituted an anti-biblical humanistic philosophy of education for the truth. The new philosophy required different teaching methods. These new methods have destroyed and wasted the minds of America's youth. As the old saying goes, "For best results follow the instructions of the manufacturer." The flip side of this is the reality that if we reject God's way of thinking we are creating our own disaster. The "dumbing down" of America is no accident. It is the direct result of the great paradigm shift from teaching methods based upon the biblical worldview to teaching methods based upon a humanistic worldview.

The chart below attempts to summarize some of the major changes of this paradigm shift in teaching methods. We will discuss its main points in the text that follows.

The Great Paradigm Shift in Teaching Methods

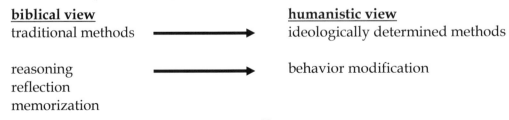

<u>biblical view</u>		<u>humanistic view</u>
traditional methods	⟶	ideologically determined methods
reasoning reflection memorization	⟶	behavior modification

| phonics | → | "look-say" reading
whole language |
| traditional math | → | "new math" of the 1960's
new "new math" of the 1990's |

Any discussion of the paradigm shift in America's teaching methods must consider the enormous influence of John Dewey (1859-1952). Dewey was an overt atheist. The intellectual establishment in America had come a long way since the time of Horace Mann. The writings of men like Karl Marx and Charles Darwin fueled the anti-biblical movement to replace the biblical worldview with a secular worldview. Whereas Mann had to show at least lip service to Christianity, by Dewey's time atheists were welcome in an intellectual world that was becoming increasingly hostile toward traditional Christianity.

Dewey was a philosopher, a prolific writer, and a signer of the original Humanist Manifesto in 1933. He was a strong believer in the philosophy of pragmatism as articulated by William James. Pragmatism says that the truth of a proposition is judged by its practical outcome. It denies universal or absolute truth. According to pragmatism, values arise in the context of human experience so that truth and values change with circumstances.

Pragmatism has become the underlying philosophy of contemporary American culture. It is commonly expressed by the overused expression, "That works for me!" Many Christians confuse pragmatism with being practical. This is unfortunate because the biblical worldview is practical, but it is the opposite of being pragmatic.

The opposite of being pragmatic is to be principled. Whereas the motive behind being pragmatic is to "get the job done by whatever way works" and has serving self as its goal, being principled means being loyal to a higher truth even if it does not serve self. Being principled involves submission to truth. If you are a Christian this means being in submission to the Word of God.

As noted earlier, the teaching methods favored by a philosophy of education are determined by that philosophy's concept of the nature of man and its concept of the nature of truth. Actually, the word, "truth," is not even in the pragmatist's vocabulary. The chart below summarizes the difference between the biblical and the humanistic view of truth.

Two Views of Truth

Biblical	Humanistic
truth	knowledge
source—God's Word	source---man's experience
absolute	relative
unchanging	changing
has authority	subject to man's use
comes from outside a man	comes from inside a man
comes by submission	comes by experience
facts are important and have authority experience	only knowledge relative to man's is valuable

Dewey's worldview was pure humanism. It was man-centered and recognized no higher authority than the human race. Spiritual reality was denied. Dewey embraced all the anti-Christian beliefs of Humanist Manifestos I and II, and he is revered by our secular culture as one of greatest minds ever to influence American education. He is most remembered as being the father of the Progressive Movement of the early twentieth century.

Some of Dewey's thinking that characterized Progressive Education was its rejection of traditional education and its emphasis on learning through experience. According to Dewey, experience is the essence of all learning, process is more important than content, and the goal of education is the socialization of the child. He, like humanistic educators before him, believed in trusting the natural inclinations of the child. He advocated child-centered classrooms where the teacher was merely a facilitator rather than an authority figure.

Dewey was a prolific writer and he made it clear that his new philosophy of education rejected traditional American education. In *Experience and Education* he wrote,

> "The rise of what is called the new education and progressive schools is of itself a product of discontent with traditional education. In effect it is a criticism of the latter. When the implied criticism is made explicit it reads somewhat as follows: The traditional scheme is, in essence, one of imposition from above and from outside. It imposes adult standards, subject matter, and methods upon those who are only growing slowly toward maturity . . .
>
> If one attempts to formulate the philosophy of education implicit in the practices of the new education, we may, I think, discover certain common principles amid the variety of progressive schools now existing. To imposition from above is opposed expression and cultivation of individuality; to external discipline is opposed free activity; to learning from texts and teachers, learning through experience; to acquisition of isolated skills and techniques by drill, is opposed acquisition of them as means of attaining ends which make direct vital appeal; to preparation for a more or less remote future is opposed making the most of the opportunities of present life; to static aims and materials is opposed acquaintance with a changing world."[37]

Dewey's influence has been a major factor in creating a negative attitude toward traditional education. This attitude reigns supreme in teacher colleges and departments of education. Even though we have not had traditional education in American schools for several generations, it still has a bad reputation among the education elite. As a matter of fact, many of the modern trends in education that are based on humanistic philosophy are incorrectly labeled "traditional education" when they fail. Chances are that we all have picked up some negative feelings toward traditional education because of the false stereotype the humanists have created. The following chart is an attempt to set the record straight by comparing this false stereotype with reality.

---

[37] John Dewey, *Experience and Education* (New York: Touchstone, 1997), 18-20.

The Anti-Traditional Education Bias

The Negative Stereotype	The Reality
mindless rote learning	emphasis on the three R's
little minds crammed with irrelevant, useless facts	content rich
cruel, rigid, authoritarian	disciplined atmosphere
narrow-minded indoctrination	conveyed the biblical worldview
unenlightened by the concepts of modern psychology	imparted healthy "Protestant" work ethic
tedious, boring experience for the child	academically much better results than modern trends
all creativity and self-expression is stifled	produced the worlds finest: --authors --inventors --statesmen --scientists

We tend to believe that "newer" means "better" and that we live in a more enlightened age than our grandfathers did. This arrogant attitude is especially strong among secular-minded educators. Our goal is not to "turn back the clock," but we do need to reevaluate our attitude toward traditional education. The form of education loosely described as traditional was far more consistent with a biblical worldview than what we have today, and an honest appraisal of its effectiveness will admit that it got far superior results than modern humanistic education does today.

Behavior Modification

As noted earlier, behavior modification is the logical choice of teaching method for those who subscribe to the beliefs of modern psychology. The chart below summarizes the differences between behavior modification and traditional methods.

Behavior Modification v. Traditional Methods

Behavior Modification	Traditional Methods
Root—Humanist Worldview	Root—Biblical Worldview
Mind—physical brain, part of a highly evolved nervous system	Mind—part of man's spiritual nature
Thinking—non-reflective associations of stimuli and responses	Thinking—a spiritual exercise

Goal—changed behavior by controlling the environment	Goal—impartation of truth
Finished Product—pre-exists in the minds of the educators and is limited to specific parameters	Finished Product—unlimited possibilities (John 8:32)

Methods:	Methods:
conditioned responses	reasoning, reflection
--multiple choice	--reading
--true or false	--lecture
--fill in the blank	--essay
--social pressure	--recitation
--external pressure	--internal inspiration

It is highly ironic that humanism, the philosophy that tries to exalt the human race, actually degrades man by denying his spirituality. The humanistic view of human behavior which is expressed in modern psychology rules out any spiritual causality in human behavior. According to modern psychology, man is no different from an animal when it comes to learning. But the Bible clearly recognizes that thinking or knowing is a spiritual exercise. I Corinthians 2:11 says, *"For what man knoweth the things of a man, save the spirit of man which is in him? Even so the things of God knoweth no man, but the Spirit of God."*

Humanistic teaching methods treat children like animals. The results are stifling. Just as no horse or dog can ever know more than his trainer, so too a child taught by behavior modification will never learn more than the predetermined outcomes in his teacher's lesson plans. Just as horses and dogs trained by behavior modification become increasingly dependent upon their trainers, so do children taught by behavior modification become increasingly dependent upon their teachers.

John 8:23 says, *"And you will know the truth, and the truth shall make you free."* The biblical worldview sees attainment of truth as the ultimate goal of education. Biblical teaching methods will serve this goal. Although as Christian educators we may have a vision in our mind as to how we would like to see our graduates behave, we are not in the business of behavior modification. Behavior modification's goal is to place children on a career path that will enable them to comfortably fit into society. Biblical education's goal is imparting truth and giving children the skills they need to seek the truth on their own. This was always the purpose of traditional education. Who are we to presume we can determine the future destiny (outcome based education) of the children God entrusts to us? Our role is to impart truth. According to the Bible there is power in the truth; it will "make you free." The possibilities for a person liberated by the truth are endless.

One of the main tasks, therefore, of biblical education is to equip a child to seek truth on his own. This means developing sound reasoning skills. One of the tragic results of modern humanistic teaching methods is that they discourage the development of sound reasoning skills. This topic will be discussed in more detail in a later section of this course.

The intent of the above comparison of behavior modification with traditional teaching methods is not to say that Christian educators should never use any of the methods listed under behavior modification. For example, we may have need from time to time to use "true or false" or "fill in the blank" questions. What we must consider is the long-term results of a constant reliance on the methods of behavior modification and a serious neglect of the traditional methods.

Traditional methods like teaching children how to write essays are hard work for the teacher. Getting children to learn to take notes from lectures is almost unheard of today. We have come a long way from the time when traditional methods characterized America's classrooms. We live in a culture of eight-second sound bites, attention deficit disorder, video games, and television. Behavior modification is definitely easier. This is always a problem with humanism. Humanism's greatest ally is man's fallen carnal nature. Turning back to traditional methods will be a battle against the grain for Christian educators, yet battle we must. Humanistic teaching methods have created a nation of sheepish consumers who no longer know how to think. Some of its bad fruit is noted in the list below.

Some Results of Humanistic Education

- The student is historically and politically ignorant, except for "politically correct" thinking.
- The student is unscholarly. He does not like to study.
- The student is peer group dependent.
- Image is more important than substance.
- Style is more important than content.
- The student tends to be highly subjective and opinionated.
- The student is consumer (not production) oriented.
- The student is unable to self-educate.
- The student lacks the necessary skills to: read, reason, communicate, make prudent decisions, lead.

The Church has not escaped these negative results of humanistic education. "Dumbed down" Christians are described in Matthew 5:13: "*Ye are the salt of the earth: but if the salt have lost his savour, wherewith shall it be salted? it is thenceforth good for nothing, but to be cast out, and to be trodden under foot of men.*" Humanistic teaching methods take the salt out of child. We must, through methods compatible with the biblical worldview, make the next generation salty again by instilling in them a love for the truth and giving them the tools to seek it. The Christian teacher who thinks her mission is confined to the four walls of her classroom is missing the big picture. We have an extremely important part to play in this great spiritual war.

Lesson 8

Biblical Teaching Methods: Part II

Goals:

1. To gain a deeper understanding of the harmful effects of humanistic teaching methods.
2. To gain a deeper appreciation for teaching methods that are based on the biblical worldview.

Assignment:

1. Read Lesson 8.
2. Write answers to Study Questions below.

Study Questions:

1. Explain why teaching is not entertaining.
2. Explain why a teacher is not merely a facilitator.
3. How is child-centered education harmful to a child?
4. How has over concern for a child's self-expression contributed to the dumbing down of America?
5. Explain how the controversy over the use of phonics is essentially a spiritual issue.

For Further Study (see resource list):

Blumenfeld, Samuel L. *NEA: The Whole Language/OBE Fraud.* Boise, ID: The Paradigm Company, 1995.

Stout, Maureen. *The Feel-Good Curriculum.* Cambridge, MA: Perseus Books, 2000.

Lesson 8

Biblical Teaching Methods: Part II

Humanistic education, as Dewey clearly stated, attempts to discredit methods that are compatible with the biblical view of education and replace them with humanistic methods. In summary:

Humanistic education . . .

Attacks	Exalts
Learning from authority	Learning by experience
Teacher-centered classrooms	Child-centered classrooms
Individual responsibility in learning	Group learning
Convention	Self-expression
Discipline	Spontaneity
Systematic, incremental approach	Random approach
Learning through work	Learning through play
Practice and drill	Incidental learning
Teacher lecture	Peer group discussion
Content	Process
Self-denial	Self-esteem
Principled Approach	Pragmatic Approach
Concepts	Images
The past	The Present
Phonics	Whole Language
Reason	Emotion
Fact	Opinion
Objective truth	Relativism
Depravity of human nature	Basic "goodness" of man
Creation	Evolution

And ultimately-
God	**Man**

Learning by Experience

One of Dewey's themes that has a death grip on our thinking about education is his emphasis on learning by experience. It is commonly held by Christian educators as well as secular educators that learning by experience is the "best way" because "children will remember it better." Before Dewey, learning by experience was not highly valued. The biblical worldview does not condone it. As a matter of fact, the biblical view is that learning by experience is the last resort for those who reject learning by accepting the counsel of those in authority. The prodigal son, for example, learned by experience. It is an ill-advised way to learn, biblically speaking.

The Bible condones learning by accepting the words of those in authority. Proverbs gives us a great example. The continual theme of Proverbs is that of a father giving instructions to his son. Throughout the book the son is exhorted to listen, to pay attention, and to heed the instructions of the father.

Please note that this criticism of the emphasis on learning by experience is not directed against learning-by-doing in the sense of practicing skills. Traditional education has always valued practice and repetitive practice known as drill. It was Dewey who opposed this kind of learning by experience. Recall his words, "To acquisition of isolated skills and techniques by drill, is opposed acquisition of them as a means of attaining ends which make direct vital appeal."[38] For Dewey and those who came after him, learning by experience meant learning by discovery.

Learning by discovery is the least efficient use of school time. This is one of the reasons modern education is so content anemic. Too much time is wasted on learning material by discovery that can be better learned by reading about it. The concept that children need to touch, smell, and taste something to learn about it is a corollary to this thinking.

The argument is frequently put forth that learning by experience is more fun for the children. This thinking stems from another mindset that has poisoned modern American education. This thinking confuses education with entertainment. It stems from the humanistic tradition that goes back to Pestalozzi and Froebel who promoted the idea of child-centered education. From the humanistic perspective "work" is a bad word. Humanists maintain that learning happens best in a play atmosphere. The teacher's role is merely to facilitate learning by ensuring a nurturing environment. The child knows best what he should learn and when he should learn it. To return to Dewey's words, "To imposition from above is opposed expression and cultivation of individuality; to external discipline is opposed free activity; to learning from texts and teachers, learning through experience."[39]

The fact that most Christian teachers are uncomfortable with the term "teacher-centered classroom" illustrates how deeply humanistic thinking has infected their thinking about education. We have even come to believe that a lot of control and direction from the teacher will harm children. Again, this illustrates how important it is that we examine our assumptions.

Work versus play

According to Webster, the word, "muse", means "to think or to meditate on." The prefix "a" creates an opposite. In essence, "amuse" means not thinking or "directing attention away from serious matters." Amusement is passive. It requires no work. Learning is not passive. It does require work. It's as simple as that.

Modern Christian parents and teachers are going to have to expend considerable deliberate effort to shake off the world's thinking when it comes to work in the classroom. We have been brainwashed by the humanists into thinking that "school should be fun" and "it is the teacher's job to make school interesting for the children." In other words, we have come to expect teachers to entertain our children.

Teaching is not entertaining.

Learning requires exertion. It is not a passive experience. Work is only a bad word when we view it from a carnal perspective. Work is not a result of the fall. God commanded Adam to *"Be fruitful, and multiply, and replenish the earth, and subdue it: and have dominion over the fish of the sea, and over the fowl of the air, and over every living thing that moveth upon the earth."*

[38] Ibid.
[39] Ibid.

(Genesis 1:28). This command was given to Adam before he sinned. Work, exertion, taking action, being active rather than passive is not part of a curse. The curse may have complicated things, but work itself is a result of our being created in the image of an active God.

The recipient of entertainment is in a passive state. Entertainment discourages exertion. The goal of a teacher should be to develop active learners. Our goal should not be to make learning "fun," but to teach children to appreciate the value of work. The best lesson they can learn is that work leads to accomplishment and accomplishment leads to satisfaction. In our culture of immediate gratification, one of the most important lessons a child can learn is the great biblical theme of deferred reward.

A teacher is not a facilitator.

The concept of the teacher as a facilitator comes out of the philosophy that a child knows best what to learn and when to learn, and that he will naturally want to learn. A facilitator is seen as an aid who comes along side of a child rather than someone who takes a directive control over the learning process. There are certainly times when a teacher does need to be seen as a helper or coach, but being a teacher is not equivalent to being a facilitator.

The mentality that a teacher should be a facilitator has so influenced our attitude that a teacher who is directive in her classroom is viewed negatively as "controlling" or "dominating." These teachers are considered old-fashioned and out-of-date. This is the anti-traditional education bias at work.

The instructions to parents and the examples of teaching given in the Bible are not of facilitators or of child-centered education. The Bible endorses direct instruction.

Child-centered education is harmful to a child.

Learning involves humility and submission to authority. One of the most important lessons a child can learn is that he is not the center of his family, nor is he the center of his classroom. If he does not learn this at an early age he will grow up thinking he is the center of the universe, which is exactly what humanism preaches. It is difficult to make good Christians out of people with this humanistic attitude.

As Christian educators we should be preparing children for life in the real world. According to the biblical worldview the real world is God-centered, not man-centered. Child-centered classrooms create self-centered children. Man must learn to live with the fact that God, not man, is the center of everything. Child-centered education is a tremendous hindrance against learning this all-important truth. Children from child-centered homes and child-centered classrooms will find it much more difficult to learn to pick up their cross daily and walk as a Christian.

The myth of "socialization."

According to Dewey the purpose of education is the socialization of the child. Before Dewey, "socialization" was not a concern for educators. When America's thinking was more influenced by the biblical worldview it was widely held that peer group influence would more likely be negative and should be kept at a minimum. Yet today even Christian parents worry that their children will not be properly socialized. This current thinking is one hundred percent humanistic and zero percent biblical. The Bible places all responsibility for education in the hands of adults, not other children. The idea that a child "needs" peer group identity is widely accepted even by Christian parents and educators, yet it has no biblical basis.

The belief that children learn best through interaction with other children is a myth. It is often argued that much learning comes through peer group discussion, but any honest teacher will tell you that very little learning comes through peer group discussion. Discussion does work, but it requires the direction of one who knows more than the students. Jesus used questions and answers, but He was in control of where the discussion went. Even Socrates, a hero of the humanists, led his students in his famous method of questions and answers that has become known as the Socratic method. But the interaction was between Socrates and one of his students, not two of his students. The real value of being in a group discussion for a child is that he can hear the interaction between other children and the teacher. Very little is gained from the meager supply of wisdom to be found in the peer group.

"Cooperative Learning"

The trend of the twentieth century has been toward "cooperative learning" or "collaborative learning." This movement has its roots in Dewey's influence. At its core its agenda is actually political. It engenders the feeling of belonging that is essential to the utopian global socialist society. It is an appeal for allegiance to the human peer group over allegiance to family, authority, truth, or God. As stated earlier, the worldview war is fundamentally a spiritual war. The influence of this trend on our culture is subliminal yet very pervasive. We have a huge problem in our culture today that some have labeled "group think." "Group think" is the habit of finding security in identifying one's thinking with the group or the contemporary trends of the culture. It is peer group dependency at its worst.

Furthermore, cooperative or collaborative projects are counter productive to learning. They waste precious classroom time. Even math today is often treated as a group problem to be solved by committee action.

One of the most devastating results of cooperative learning is that it discourages excellence. Group projects are often given a single group grade that fails to recognize the difference in effort and understanding of the various individuals in the group. Excellence goes unrewarded while laziness or shoddy work often gets a free ride.

A more subtle but no less detrimental result of cooperative learning is the eroding of respect for authority. We live in the era of call-in talk radio where listeners are urged to call the radio station to express their opinions on the air. The implication is that every opinion is as good as every other. Self-expression becomes the preoccupation rather than arriving at truth. But every opinion is not as good as every other. Some opinions deserve more respect than others. A heavy reliance on peer group discussion and self-expression give children a false sense of the importance of their views and it tends to erode respect for opinions that are based on fact and expertise. As a result, children fail to gain a healthy respect for expertise, experience, age, and maturity.

Teacher Lecture

Modern teacher-training textbooks take a dim view of teacher lecture. Most adults carry in their minds a negative stereotype of lecture as a dry and boring experience. Very few teachers below the college level lecture. It is considered outmoded and ineffective.

Yet lecture is the most efficient teaching method. Jesus used lecture more than any other method. A good portion of the book of Proverbs is a father lecturing his son. All preaching is basically lecture. Serious graduate students will pay good money to hear knowledgeable professors lecture. Why then has lecture been given such a bad reputation?

As mentioned earlier, we live in a culture that expects to be entertained. Classroom teachers are expected to make content "fun." Christians even choose their local church based on the ability of the pastor to deliver entertaining sermons week after week. Recently television's

History Channel had a billboard advertisement showing a picture of George Washington wearing a big red clown nose with the byline, "We make history fun." We approach learning passively believing it is the responsibility of the teacher or preacher to capture our interest by their entertaining style. We have come to value style more than content. Thus lecture, unless it comes with an increasingly entertaining style, is considered boring and criticized as poor teaching.

Add to this the fact that modern children (and adults) have very short attention spans when compared to children of other times in history. Today we live in an atmosphere of fast paced visuals, super-action movies, lighting reaction video games, and constant audio and visual stimulation. Whether we want to admit it or not, we are a generation of couch potatoes lying around waiting for the next titillation.

This modern cultural atmosphere has made lecture unpopular. Most people think lecture is a bad way to teach. The majority of Christian parents and teachers share the secular culture's attitude toward lecture. Many would say it is impossible to use lecture as an effective teaching method given our modern cultural attitudes.

Without a doubt, reintroducing lecture (as well as other traditional teaching methods) into the classroom will be an uphill battle. But the alternative is worse. We are on a downhill slide commonly known as the "dumbing down of America." We can give up and let the culture dictate our standards or we can take a stand and speak truth to the culture.

There is an obvious age appropriateness that must be taken into consideration when we use lecture. We are not advocating long monologues on abstract content for small children. We need to shed the image of lecture as method only used for abstract or philosophical subjects. Jesus mixed in stories, or parables, into his lecture. Lecture does not have to be long, and it can be injected into the classroom at different times for different purposes. It works well when it is mixed with teacher interaction with the students. Some teachers use lecture this way but do not call it lecture because the word "lecture" is taboo to professional educators. We believe "lecture" is a good word and refuse to bow to the cultural negative stigma by calling it something else. Teachers should not be afraid of using direct instruction and asserting control over the learning process. We believe teacher control of the classroom is the best way to insure maximum learning in a given time.

Most people today think a child's attention span is physiological and unchangeable. They fail to recognize that it is mainly a character issue. Attention span is not only changeable, it is greatly affected by the expectations of parents and teachers. We may have to persuade parents to raise their expectations on their own children.

Lecture presupposes teacher comprehension of the content. This may put a burden on some teachers who have previously subscribed to the "facilitator" philosophy. The facilitator is supposed to be an aid to a child in his pursuit of knowledge, but not be a source of knowledge herself. This philosophy has contributed to the earlier mentioned "knowledge anemia" in modern American schools. A teacher should have mastery over the content of the grade level and subject she teaches. Christian teachers should throw away their child psychology books and read more books on history, geography, literature, and the Bible.

Character issues versus ability issues

Before modern psychology became the norm for child rearing and teaching in America, standards of behavior in the classroom were much higher. When the Bible was our standard, children were expected to respect their teachers and to sit attentively in the classroom. The common understanding was that biblical standards actually were "one size fits all." In other words, "thou shalt not steal" applied equally to all personality types and all cultural backgrounds, and yes, even to those children who had bad experiences in their early childhood.

This was a time when character issues were not confused with ability issues. For example, careless spelling, punctuation, capitalization, and penmanship were treated as character issues. They were subject to discipline because teachers (and most parents) recognized the difference between lack of effort and lack of ability. Obviously, children who were just learning how to write were not disciplined for laziness when they misspelled words, but teachers and parents were much more inclined to recognize the truth when it came to laziness and carelessness.

Human nature is the same today as it was a hundred years ago. It is just that a hundred years ago we recognized the depravity of fallen human nature in our children and had the courage to discipline them. Today we have exchanged biblical principles for the excuses offered by modern psychology and choose to coddle our children instead of lovingly disciplining them. Instead of recognizing carelessness, laziness, lack of diligence, and lack of attentiveness as character issues, we excuse our children by calling lack of character lack of ability.

In the end, character affects achievement. A gifted child with poor self-control will usually be an underachiever. On the other hand, a child with average ability with strong character will do well. The subject matter and skills that make up the content of grades one through eight (and some of us would say grades one through twelve) should be fairly easily mastered by the child of average and even somewhat below average ability. What we need to do is quit calling misbehavior "disability" and hold to higher standards for diligence, effort, and attentiveness.

The sacred cow of self-expression

Modern humanistic education has made self-expression a sacred cow. Self-expression is valued above all else and must be protected from all perceived threats. Any teaching practice that is seen as a threat to self-expression is attacked viciously. For example, the teacher who insists on correct spelling, punctuation, and grammar is criticized for stifling creativity. It is widely believed that if a child has to follow the conventions of the written language he will feel confined and bogged down with rules which will hinder his free expression. All forms of structure and convention are seen as restrictive to the development of a child's creativity. Again, we can thank Rousseau, Pestalozzi, Froebel, and many after them for this false belief which is held by modern educators with a religious fervor. And don't forget Dewey's dichotomy, "To imposition from above is opposed expression and the cultivation of individuality; to external discipline is opposed free activity;"[40]

Most Christian educators recognize this trend in its extreme. For example, we do not subscribe to the "creative spelling" that allows a child to break all the rules of the English language. Generally speaking Christian schools hold higher standards for spelling when compared to today's secular schools. The problem is that today's secular schools make a poor point of comparison. Cultural standards for writing have sunk to a new low. High school graduates today write so poorly today that employers spend millions of dollars every year on remedial courses for their employees. Even college graduates show low regard for the conventions of spelling and grammar. We live in a culture that has bought into this humanistic error that says self-expression is sacred and the conventions of written language are old-

---

[40] Ibid.

fashioned and outmoded. This is the spirit of humanism which says, "My self-expression is supreme; I don't have to submit my writing to anybody's rules."

The rules of conventional writing do not stifle creativity. A child's creativity is actually stunted, not enhanced, when we fail to teach him the basic rules of convention for writing.

The same is true for music, art, and virtually all subjects. The sacrifice of learning basic conventions and principles in the name of protecting creativity has been one of the main causes of the dumbing down of American education. Children who cannot spell and punctuate will not become great writers. Children who do not know the rudiments of music will not become great musicians. As noted earlier, during the era of traditional education with its emphasis on the rules of writing and grammar, America was not lacking in producing creative genius.

Systematic versus random approach

Another part of Dewey's dichotomy states, "to acquisition of isolated skills and techniques by drill is opposed acquisition of them as means of attaining ends which make direct vital appeal." By "ends which make direct vital appeal" Dewey means that a child should be allowed to learn what he, the child, perceives as valuable to him.

Children should be taught why they need to learn what they are learning. However, whether a child understands that he needs to learn something, or whether he agrees that he needs to learn something, is not the determining factor as to whether he should be taught. Dewey believed that the child should determine what he learns and when he learns it based upon the child's perception of its importance.

Dewey's thinking has led to the modern trend to teach with a random approach to subject matter. By random approach we mean the child's interests are the main determiner as to what is learned and when it is learned. It could be compared to a cow grazing in the pasture. If something looks good, he might take a bite out of it, if not he passes it up. It is free-range "education" instead of directed education.

The problem with this approach should be obvious. Children simply don't know what is good for them. The random approach is a very inefficient use of class time. All sorts of trivial pursuits are justified as "learning experiences." Children might have fun learning how to make pioneer porridge, but meanwhile they don't learn that Patrick Henry's Christian beliefs greatly influenced the founding of America.

We advocate a systematic approach to teaching. All subjects in the school curriculum have identifiable fundamental principles or rudiments. The most efficient way to teach content is to teach these first principles. Children who understand the rudiments of a subject are equipped to master it. Not every bit of information on a subject is equally valuable. A systematic approach separates the important from the unimportant and presents it in an orderly manner. The very experience of learning systematically is good for children. The teacher's method gives them a model for organizing their own thinking. On the other hand, the random approach produces bad thinking habits, or another way of putting it is, a scattered approach produces scatterbrains.

The difference between phonics and the whole-language philosophy for the teaching of reading is the epitome of the conflict between a systematic and a random approach. It will be discussed in more detail later.

Process versus content

One of the negative stereotypes the progressive movement pinned on traditional education was that children were learning a great quantity of content information that was irrelevant. If fault can be found with traditionalists on this issue, it is not because the information taught was irrelevant. The word "relevant" has been redefined by modern humanists. To Dewey and his followers, "relevant" means something that the child has a felt interest in. Traditionally "relevant" means material important to a child's education. The content in the traditional curriculum was much more relevant than today's humanistic content. We would say learning about George Washington is relevant because it is important to a child's understanding of American history. Humanistic history books contain more references to the Beatles and Marilyn Monroe than to George Washington because it better fits their definition of "relevant."

Relevancy can be a problem when teachers teach material without a clear understanding themselves as to why it is part of the curriculum. This happens when teachers become mere implementers of a curriculum and have no clear philosophy of education that explains why certain content is part of the curriculum. If content material is not relevant to a teacher, how can she impress upon her students that it is relevant? This underscores the importance of every teacher having a clear biblical philosophy of education. We need to know not just how to teach. We need to know why we teach what we teach.

The result of Dewey's contention that traditional education overwhelmed children with masses of irrelevant information has been a negative attitude toward the learning of content. The prevailing modern attitude is that content is not important; it's the process that counts. This attitude permeates our culture. We hear reference to religion in the phrase, "It's not what you believe, it's how sincerely you hold your beliefs that counts." And in education we continually hear, "The correct answer is not important, it's the process that counts."

One of the most detrimental consequences of this attitude is that it promotes relativism. For example, in reference to religion this attitude declares that the content of your religion is not important. You cannot claim you both believe the Bible and agree with this attitude. Content is extremely important. Process is meaningless without content. There is no believing if there is no object of belief. The correct answer is very important.

Process is important, but it is useless if it does not lead us to the right answers. We see this in the humanist philosophy of drug education and sex education. This philosophy comes from the "values clarification" thinking of Sidney Simon and company. The whole emphasis is on the process of weighing possible consequences. What the children decide about the use of drugs is not seen as important as the process of thinking about it. It does not seem to matter to the humanists that the "values clarification" method does not reduce drug use. To them it's the process that counts.

Christian teachers should avoid the pitfall of downplaying the correct answer. It is good for children to understand why they work math problems in a certain way, for example. But we cannot sacrifice accuracy for a false sense of the importance of process.

Self-esteem versus self-denial

The self-esteem movement got its start in the 1950's and 1960's through the influence of psychologists Abraham Maslow and Carl Rogers. (See Lesson 6). The influence of this unbiblical philosophy on American society has been overwhelming. Christians seem to be under this influence as much as nonbelievers. Parents and teachers have become obsessed with the fear of damaging children's self-esteem. Teachers are afraid to give out low grades or make negative critical comments on a child's work because of the possible harm to the child's self-esteem. Anything with a hint of competition has been eliminated from the curriculum. All critique of a child's progress must be stated in "positive" terms. Self-esteem has become the all-encompassing goal of parenting and schooling.

Some Christian parents and teachers are aware of the extremes of the self-esteem movement, but they do not realize how much they, themselves, have accepted the basic assumptions of the movement.

Maslow's theory that a person cannot give of himself until his own need of self-esteem is met is in direct conflict with biblical principle. The Bible preaches the exact opposite. (Matthew 6:33 and 16:24-25). Jesus was the ultimate example of self-denial. Children who are not taught to deny themselves as children will not automatically inherit this character trait at age eighteen or twenty-one. They must be taught the reason for self-denial and trained in the practice of it from an early age. Christian schools that claim to develop Christian character in their students while they subscribe to the tenets of the self-esteem movement are in serious self-contradiction.

Phonics versus Whole Language

For the last several generations in America there has been an ongoing feud over the proper way to teach reading. Although it may seem to some of us that this conflict has been going on forever, it is relatively new. For the first three centuries of American history, phonics was the consensus among parents and educators. Our first textbooks, *The New England Primer* and Noah Webster's "blue backed speller" used a phonetic approach to teach reading.

Phonics is the branch of linguistics that deals with the sounds of speech and their production, combination, description, and representation by written symbols. Phonics is based upon the fact that the written English language is a graphic representation of the sounds of words. Letters, alone or in combination, represent the different sounds, or phonemes, of the English language. It is common today to hear the statement, "English is not a phonetic language." This is not true. It is true that there are words in the English language that seem to break the rules of phonics or are difficult to decipher in terms of phonics, but these are exceptions and they occur much more infrequently than the enemies of phonics are willing to admit.

Languages like those of the ancient Egyptians or the Chinese are examples of non-phonetic written languages. These people did not use written symbols to represent sounds. Instead their writing represents ideas or concepts by transcribing symbols that suggest objects or actions. In many cases these writing systems started out as picture languages. These people's first written "language" was a string of pictures. In time they discovered shortcuts and developed symbols that came to represent common actions and objects that could be combined to tell a story. The main issue here is whether a written language attempts to represent sounds or concepts. Phonetic written languages represent sounds.

Historically the feud over the use of phonics has become one between conservative "traditionalists" who prefer phonics and liberal "progressives" who continue to find something wrong with phonics and regularly propose alternative schemes for the teaching of reading. Some of the alternatives to phonics proposed in the last seventy-five years have been labeled the "whole word," the "look-say," and the "whole language" approach. For the most part, each of these alternatives has had the life cycle of a fad. They are presented and received with a lot of excitement, they fail to teach reading, and they end up discredited as an effective way to teach reading. Each new approach promises to rectify the shortcomings of not only phonics, but those of the last failed fad. What often gets overlooked is the common thread that underlies all of the anti-phonic approaches. All the anti-phonics movements share the humanistic worldview.

For example, the most recent movement, "whole language," was imposed upon California's public schools by law in 1987. The state's reading scores plummeted. By the mid 1990's the state board of education had to admit that whole language was not working. You would think that California would have learned to mistrust modern trends in the teaching of reading. Although it was obvious that whole language did not work in California, and in fact virtually all the empirical evidence demonstrates the failure of whole language[41], California and secular educators in general refuse to return to systematic phonics. This is because systematic phonics does not fit into their humanistic worldview.

The anti-phonics trends are all branches that stem from the same anti-traditional education mindset. As noted earlier, this attitude gained great impetus from the progressive movement of Dewey's time. In the 1950's the "look-say" method was the fad. In 1955 Rudolf Flesch came out with his celebrated book, *Why Johnny Can't Read*, which drew national attention to the shortcomings of the "look-say" method. Flesch did a credible job of making the case for phonics. The general public took note, but the secular education establishment continued to ignore the evidence in favor of phonics, and twenty-six years later Flesch published a second book entitled *Why Johnny Still Can't Read*. The anti-phonics mindset is persistent because it is based on presuppositions, not on empirical evidence.

What are these presuppositions? First, it should be noted that the philosophical basis for the anti-phonics movement rarely gets exposed. Most of the anti-phonics methods, like most other humanistic trends in education, are presented on a superficial level that is more emotional than intellectual. Whole language advocates, for example, have hundreds of books and seminars that basically appeal to the unexamined presuppositions that already exist in the thinking of the majority of the teachers in this country. Typically, whole language is presented as fun and exciting for the children. Creativity is often the sacred cow that whole languages promise to protect and nourish. Traditional systematic phonics is portrayed as restrictive, stifling to creativity, and damaging to self-esteem. Whole language seminar leaders tend to be high-energy motivational speakers who promise to make life easier for teachers by eliminating the drudgery of forcing children to memorize the rules of phonics.

For those of you that are unfamiliar with whole language, it is a theory of learning to read that believes children learn to read much in the same way they learn to talk. Children learn to talk just be being around people who are talking. No formal systematic process is needed. This theory says that children will learn to read by being around good literature. They should have stories read to them and an abundance of books in proximity. The reading process, says whole language, is a trial-and-error discovery process that decodes words by using various cues that the written language presents. A child determines the meaning of a passage by responding to these cues. Syntax, the pattern of words found in sentences and phrases, is one of these cues. Semantics is another. Even the pictures on the page of a book are considered as legitimate cues in a child's process of determining the meaning of a passage.

What are some of the presuppositions of the whole language philosophy? (Note that we will be using the term "whole language" as a general term for the common philosophy that underlies the anti-phonics movement.) For starters the whole language philosophy rejects the fact that English is a phonetic language. To say English is a phonetic language is to say that written English is a representation of spoken English. It implies that the written is dependent upon the oral. In contrast whole language says, "In a whole language perspective, it is not just oral language that counts as language. Oral language, written language, sign language---each

---

[41] For abundant documentation of research verifying the superiority of phonics visit the website of The National Right to Read Foundation at www.nrrf.org.

of these is a system of linguistic conventions for creating meanings. That means none is 'the basis' for the other; none is a secondary representation of the other."[42] This view, of course, undermines the whole approach of phonics.

The above example is merely the tip of the philosophic iceberg. Whole language is based upon fundamental presuppositions about man, the world, and the meaning of reality that are the antithesis of the biblical worldview. By now it may have occurred to you that this is a deep subject that goes beyond the scope of this course. We highly recommend further study in this area, especially for primary grade teachers. Author Sam Blumenfeld has a good book on the subject entitled *The Whole Language/OBE Fraud*. To get an explanation of whole language from the anti-phonics point of view we recommend reading (cautiously) *Whole Language: What's the Difference?* See our resources section. The following quote from that book gives us a glimpse of the radically different worldview that underlies whole language:

> "From a whole language perspective, reading (and language use in general) is a process of generating hypotheses in a meaning-making transaction in a socio-historical context. As a transactional process (Rosenblatt 1978; Goodman 1984), reading is not a matter of 'getting the meaning' from a text, as if that meaning were in the text waiting to be decoded by the reader. Rather, reading is a matter of readers using the cues print provides and the knowledge they bring with them (of language subsystems, of the world) to construct a unique interpretation.

> Moreover, that interpretation is situated: reader's *creations* (not retrievals) of meaning with the text vary, depending on their purposes for reading and the expectations of others in the reading event. This view of reading implies that there is no single "correct" meaning for a given text, only plausible meanings. This view is in direct contrast to the model of reading underlying most reading instruction and evaluation."[43]

No kidding! It is also in direct contrast to the biblical worldview. Imagine what would happen to biblical truth if we read the Bible the way whole language views reading. The view expressed in this quotation comes from a modern philosophy known as constructivism. Constructivism holds that there is no such thing as an objective world, but rather only individual interpretations of reality.

"This is constructivism: the view that knowledge is not just 'out there' in the world in a vacuum, waiting for us to find it, but is created through the interaction of individuals in a given context. In constructivism 'reality' is a function of our interactions with others; together we 'construct' the world. The main difference between this perspective and the realist perspective is that constructivists do not believe there is a world that exists independently of our perspective, whereas the realist would say that there is indeed a world out there."[44]

This philosophy is enslaved to the spirit of humanism. As noted earlier, the worldview war is essentially a spiritual war. It is no accident that Christian educators have historically tended to favor phonics over whole language.

Unfortunately, Christian education's preference for phonics is not as strong and clear as it should be. Many Christian educators are confused and under the influence of secular thinking when it comes to teaching reading. Education departments at Christian colleges

---

[42] Atwerger, Edelsky, and Flores. *Whole Language: What's the Difference?* (Portsmouth, N.H.: Heinemann, 1991), 9.
[43] Ibid., 19-20
[44] Maureen Stout. *The Feel-Good Curriculum*, (New York: Perseus Books, 2000), 258.

advocate elements of the whole language philosophy. Christian school associations often host seminars by whole language advocates, and many Christian schoolteachers and home schooling parents have bought into the whole language philosophy.

To make things more confused we have the phenomena of "lip service" phonics. Whole language programs have failed so miserably that there has been a general reaction by parents and the public. We predict that "whole language" as the label for the anti-phonics movement will soon be obsolete and the movement will have to come up with a new name. This has been their history, and there is no evidence that they have learned their lesson and have abandoned their fundamental philosophy. They remain committed to the removal of phonics from the teaching of reading, but sometimes the pressure of public opinion causes them to make superficial concessions. In recent years whole language advocates have talked about incorporating phonics into their system. Since philosophically whole language is anathema to phonics, any use of "phonics" in a whole language sense would necessarily be superficial, thus we call it "lip service" phonics. An example of this would be the superficial use of first letter sounds as done on the TV show, "Sesame Street."

Real phonics is systematic and incremental. It is the practice of teaching all the fundamental rules of the written language with the intention of giving the child the tools to master the reading process. To the degree we use elements of the whole language philosophy we risk impairing a child's ability to read.

For the purposes of this course our message is this. Examine both your practices and your underlying assumptions about the teaching of reading. All methods are not equal. Methods that are compatible with a biblical worldview will work in the real world. Methods that are not compatible will contribute to the dumbing down of America.

Developing Sound Reasoning Skills

Goals:

1. To gain a deeper appreciation of the importance of developing sound reasoning skills in children.
2. To gain a deeper understanding of teaching practices that help develop sound reasoning skills.

Assignment:

1. Read Lesson 9.
2. Write answers to Study Questions below.

Study Questions:

1. Why is the restoration of reasoning skills important to developing a biblical worldview?
2. How does the traditional concept of separate subject "disciplines" contribute to the development of sound reasoning skills?
3. How does the use of systematic phonics contribute to the development of sound reasoning skills?
4. How do whole language methods cause "learning disabilities"?
5. How is the over use of images detrimental to the development of sound reasoning skills?
6. Explain why sound reasoning is more an issue of discipline than intelligence.

For Further Study (see resource list):

Postman, Neil. *Amusing Ourselves to Death.* New York: Penguin Books, 1985.

Sykes, Charles J. *Dumbing Down Our Kids.* New York: St. Martin's Press, 1995.

Lesson 9

Developing Sound Reasoning Skills

"The first of seven famous debates between Abraham Lincoln and Stephen A. Douglas took place on August 21, 1858, in Ottawa, Illinois. Their arrangements provided that Douglas would speak first, for one hour; Lincoln would take an hour and a half to reply; Douglas, a half hour to rebut Lincoln's reply. This debate was considerably shorter than those to which the two men were accustomed. In fact, they had tangled several times before, and all of their encounters had been much lengthier and more exhausting. For example, on October 16, 1854, in Peoria, Illinois, Douglas delivered a three-hour address to which Lincoln, by agreement, was to respond. When Lincoln's turn came, he reminded the audience that it was already 5 p.m., that he would probably require as much time as Douglas, and that Douglas was still scheduled for a rebuttal. He proposed, therefore, that the audience go home, have dinner, and return refreshed for four more hours of talk. The audience amiably agreed, and matters proceeded as Lincoln had outlined.

"What kind of audience was this? Who were these people who could so cheerfully accommodate themselves to seven hours of oratory? It should be noted, by the way, that Lincoln and Douglas were not presidential candidates; at the time of their encounter in Peoria they were not even candidates for the United States Senate. But their audiences were not especially concerned with their official status. These were people who regarded such events as essential to their political education, who took them to be an integral part of their social lives, and who were quite accustomed to extended oratorical performances. Typically at county or state fairs, programs included speakers, most of who were allotted three hours for their arguments. And since it was preferred that speakers not go unanswered, their opponents were allotted an equal length of time."[45]

America is Losing Its Mind

In his insightful book, *Amusing Ourselves to Death*, Neil Postman gives us the above illustration that reveals a modern cultural crisis. America is losing its mind. America is losing its ability to think. America is losing its desire to think. This is a national crisis that has catastrophic consequences.

Consider how we elect our public officials. Just a century and a half ago we rationally considered issues. Today men and women are elected based upon their ability to create an appealing public image. Slogans have replaced rational debate. Image has replaced substance. Clever TV commercials that appeal to prejudices and emotions have replaced rational discussion of the issues

And then there is the phenomena called "reality TV." There is absolutely nothing real about "reality TV," yet American viewers don't care. We don't desire the truth. We prefer to live in a world of self-deceptive fantasy. We don't want to think. We prefer to be entertained.

Many Christians are concerned about the moral crisis in American culture, and rightly so. We get worried when there is an economic crisis, and we get upset when a social crisis like violence in the public schools comes close to us. Yet most of us are hardly aware that there is an intellectual crisis.

---

[45] Neil Postman, *Amusing Ourselves to Death* (New York: Penguin Books, 1985), 44.

The consequences of this intellectual crisis are monumental. When a nation stops thinking it is ready for its downfall. The Adolf Hitlers of the world are waiting in the wings. A nation that loses its ability to think will soon and certainly lose its liberty. The ability to reason is fundamental to the future of the church and the nation. Without the ability to reason, both the American church and the nation have tragedy in their future.

This intellectual crisis, however, is not independent of the moral crisis. Our loss of ability to reason is a consequence of sin. The dumbing down of America is the fruit of disobedience. We have rejected the truth of the Bible and built our philosophies of education upon humanism. These philosophies are bound to bear bad fruit.

The Restoration of Reasoning

God is a God of order. Logic is the natural law of thinking that God created so He could have common ground to communicate with us, we with Him, and we with each other. Logic is not the invention of Aristotle. It is a gift from God. The human mind functions and thrives under this law of logic.

When the Bible says, *"Come now, and let us reason together,"* (Isaiah 1:18), it implies we can reason. As a matter of fact, the Bible expects us to reason. The Bible is a book of principles, of fundamental truths. The Bible does not give us detailed instructions for every possible life situation. It gives us principles and expects us to use our reasoning ability to reason from the universal principles to particular applications. In the image of God we were created with the capacity to reason, and in several places in the Bible we are commanded to reason, reflect, and meditate. See Isaiah 1:18, II Timothy 2:7, Joshua 1:8, and Psalms 1:2.

By now you may be getting the message that the failure of Christian schools to impart a biblical worldview is not just an issue of content, but also very much an issue teaching methods. The restoration of the biblical worldview in Christian education cannot happen without a restoration of sound reasoning skills, and the restoration of sound reasoning skills can only happen if we return to teaching methods based upon the biblical philosophy of education.

Strategies for Developing Sound Reasoning Skills

Behavior modification bypasses mental reflection. It is essentially learning by association. Pavlov's dog learned to salivate upon hearing the ringing of a bell because the sound of the bell had become linked by association to the sight and smell of meat. This type of response has been appropriately labeled "knee jerk" response. When a stimulus like a rubber hammer hits your knee, your leg will automatically kick outward. Thinking never enters into the process.

Teaching methods advocated by modern humanistic education are predominantly forms of behavior modification. Much of it focuses on emotion. In teachers' guides, for example, suggested questions for use in classroom discussion frequently begin with the phrase, "How do you feel about (such and such)?" Although lip service is paid to "critical thinking skills" and "higher order thinking," very little is done in modern secular education to encourage rational reflection. In fact, modern humanistic methods cause passivity, mental laziness, and the destruction of the ability to reason. The ultimate fruit of this kind of education is a nation of gullible sheep that can be manipulated by the glitzy advertisements of Madison Avenue or the smooth talk of slick politicians.

If we want the students from our Christian schools to graduate with a true biblical worldview, we must not only present content from a biblical worldview, we must teach them how to reason logically. The remainder of this lesson is a description of strategies to develop sound reasoning skills in your students.

1.   Be systematic in presenting concepts and subject matter.

We live in the era known as the information age. In fact, we live in a time of information overload. It is easy to get overwhelmed by the constant barrage of data that is poured on us each day by advertising, the media, education, government regulations, and the Internet. This is one area where there is no turning back the clock. We must learn to cope. We can't take in all the data, so we need a way to sort it out. In other words, we need a system.

We use various methods to deal with data physically. We use file folders, color-coding, alphabetical order, and numbering systems, just to name a few. It is a matter of survival. If we don't have a system, things get out of control. We need a way to control the information that comes our way on paper or digitally. Even more importantly, we need a way to control the information that we receive mentally.

Many people do not experience the feeling of information overload because they rely on other people to screen and sort information for them. This is true for children to one degree or another. Christian parents, for example, will prevent their children from viewing pornography on the Internet.

The problem is that modern American adults are becoming increasingly dependent on others to screen and sort information for them. In essence they are letting others do their thinking for them.

For example, a growing number of Americans let television do their thinking for them. If it was advertised on TV, they will buy it. If it is the opinion of the network news anchorperson, they accept it. If it is the sexual norm of the trendiest sit-com, they will make it their norm too. Instead of developing a systematic way to handle incoming data we are increasingly becoming dependent upon the media, our college professors, the federal government, or the latest opinion polls to do our thinking for us.

Most Christians would agree that we should not let the world determine our values (though this is increasingly the case). We would say something like, "A Christian is not to follow the ways of the world." We tend to think about this as a "spiritual" issue rather than an intellectual one. This reveals a chronic problem with the modern American Church. We tend to separate the "spiritual" from the rest of life. We tell our young people to follow the Bible instead of the world, but we fail to give them important skills that can help them do it. "How to think," we say, "is an intellectual issue. Since it is not spiritual, it's neutral. Therefore we can leave it to the secular experts. They can teach our children how to think."

This mentality has greatly weakened the influence of the modern Christianity on American culture. Furthermore it has handicapped our young people by sending them out into the world ill-equipped to handle the pressures and temptations of the world. By separating life into the "spiritual," which usually means matters of personal salvation, and the "secular," which usually means everything else, we have abdicated much of life to the authority of the secular experts. We need to return to the worldview that sees the Bible as the definitive authority over all areas of life and erase this false division between the sacred and the secular. For the issue at hand, this means overcoming the mentality that creates this artificial division between the "spiritual" and the intellectual.

To be systematic means to have some criteria, standards, or principles from which to judge whether something is of value or not. From the biblical perspective these criteria are not man-made, but are God's principles which are found in the Bible. To have a system means to be constantly referring back to this criteria. The Bible says we are to judge all things (1 Cor 2:15). This is real "critical thinking."

Let us consider the study of history as an example. How do we decide what to put into the world history curriculum and what to leave out? We need criteria to determine what is of importance and what is not. We need a system. The humanists will refer to their worldview to find their criteria.

Christians should turn to principles in the Bible. If the Bible teaches us that history is the record of God fulfilling his purposes in time, then we should prioritize those events that best illustrate this truth. We should arrange this data for presentation in a way that will underscore our main point.

If our worldview is humanistic we will see history as a random bag of circumstances in which man is evolving into a higher form of life. Or we may see history as the glorious struggle of the human spirit to assert itself. Or we may see history like Karl Marx did, as the record of the struggle of economic forces. Or we may see history as the struggle for women's liberation. How ever we interpret history will determine what data we choose to teach and how we present it. This is exactly what the humanists are doing in public education.

To teach systematically means to have a clear understanding of why we teach what we are teaching. Much of today's teaching is unsystematic.

For example, the thematic unit approach to curriculum tends to be unsystematic. In this approach, the glue that holds the unit together is a theme, not a clear set of principles. Typically the thematic unit approach is "cross-curricular." A common theme of content is chosen as the unifying focus for all the traditional subjects for a given time. The theme becomes the driving force rather than any system. For example, if the theme were "American frontier life," a teacher might have her class study this era in history, read *Little House on the Prairie* in literature, make homemade bread for science class, and count cowboys and Indians in math. Instead of using the traditional division of subject matter, the theme becomes the constant, and each of the traditional subjects is forced to fit the theme.

We used to call the traditional subject divisions "disciplines." This is based upon the notion that there are basic principles for math, music, science, language, etc., that the student needs to come to respect, learn, and eventually master.

Today we live in an era that exalts spontaneity, intuitiveness, subjectivity, and emotion. Objectivity, rational discourse, and logic are neglected and disparaged. Some see this as an issue of the "left-brain" tendency versus the "right-brain" tendency or the masculine temperament versus the feminine temperament. What ever you want to call it, our culture and our educational practices have gotten way out of balance. Developing sound reasoning skills in our students will mean going against cultural trends and perhaps our own tendencies or preferences.

The secret to teaching systematically is to first develop the habit of thinking systematically. The teacher must be systematic internally before she can be systematic externally. The old adage that example is the best teacher applies here. We teach our students to think systematically both by example and by direct instruction.

Alternatives to being systematic are to be spontaneous or random or even whimsical. There are times when even being whimsical might be appropriate in the classroom. Our point is that in general modern educational practices need to be severely adjusted toward being more systematic.

2. Use systematic phonics to teach reading.

Learning to read is the first major intellectual task in a young child's life. How he is taught will make an impression that will have tremendous impact on his personal intellectual development for years to come. It is important that the teacher understand that the method she chooses to instruct the child will become a model for him to imitate. This is not just an issue of learning to read. It's an issue of how a child will tackle intellectual challenges in the future. If he is taught to read randomly, he will have been denied an important example of systematic thinking.

The written English language is a phonetic representation of the spoken English language. The set of symbols that represent the sounds of the language is our alphabet. Dr. Miriam Balmuth, in her scholarly work, *The Roots of Phonics*, discusses the advantage of an alphabetic writing system:

"A feature of the alphabetic writing system that sets it dramatically apart from the preceding systems is the small number of characters it requires. Since there are considerably fewer phonemes in any spoken language than there are ideas, words, or syllables, many fewer characters are needed in alphabetic writing than in the writing systems that symbolize those more complex linguistic units. Thus, there were a total of about 600 logographic and syllabic signs in the most recent Sumerian writing, about 700 in the Egyptian, and more than 450 in the Hittite, while the letters of the various alphabets have characteristically totaled between twenty and thirty-five. Furthermore, with the passage of time, the older systems tended to acquire many determinatives and additional markings to clarify the meanings of individual symbols, causing the systems to become increasingly cumbersome.

Another striking characteristic of the alphabetic system, one that relates to learning how to read it, is the fact that, after the relatively few symbols of a particular language have been mastered, any reader can thereafter, theoretically, unlock independently all the written words in that language. That independence was a crucial departure from the earlier systems, which require every new reader to depend on others to provide the key for each of the numerous symbols. This feature may also have been an important stimulus for the adoption of alphabetic systems by so much of the literate world."[46]

Teaching a child the principles or rules of phonics is giving him the tools of mastery over the written language. Phonics gives him an understanding of the purpose of the alphabet and the knowledge of how to use it. Learning the sound-letter correspondence gives a child the keys to reading and writing. More from Dr. Balmuth:

"In a classically structured alphabetic system, a different written character is assigned to each phoneme in the spoken language. For writing purposes, therefore, each word to be recorded must be separated into the speech sounds of which it is composed. The characters for those speech sounds are then set down in the same sequence in which they are produced in the spoken word. The reader of such a system must perceive each character in turn, blend their sounds in strict sequence, and so reconstruct the original word.

This procedure would be tedious for a written selection of any length if a fortunate process did not generally take place. That is, with repeated experience, the string of characters seems eventually to be perceived as a whole unit—almost as a logogram—making the process a good deal easier than it would be if every word had to be sounded out anew each time. Exactly how this occurs is not yet clear. There is evidence that, despite this apparently unified

---

[46] Miriam Balmuth, *The Roots of Phonics* (Timonium, MD: York Press, 1982), 31.

perception, the blending of individual units continues to take place, although at an extremely rapid rate."[47]

In other words, even when experienced readers are reading at a rapid rate, they are still processing words letter by letter in a linear sequence. When we read we are seeing letters, not whole words. Our minds, at speeds faster than our best computers, are using the principles of phonics every time we read.

The consequence of humanistic methods

Chapter one of the book of Romans describes the degeneration of the human mind that comes as a result of sin. When men refuse to honor God the consequence is a depraved mind (Romans 1:28). When men reject God's revealed truth, they are left to their own feeble wits to invent a substitute explanation for life and reality. Paul says that men ought to see the truth about God when they observe his creation (Romans 1:20), but they don't. Sin corrupts man's ability to see truth.

When men embrace false philosophies, they lose their ability to see reality. There is no better example of this than the anti-phonics movement.

Phonics is common sense, yet the humanists are so blinded by their ideology that they not only fail to see the obvious appropriateness of phonics, they vigorously oppose the use of phonics. Unfortunately, this is not merely an academic disagreement. The use of whole language methods to teach reading has severe negative consequences. We believe whole language approaches to teaching reading not only produce illiteracy, they cause "learning disabilities."

Reading and "Learning Disabilities"

A major point of contention between the biblical worldview and the humanistic worldview is the issue of causality. According to the humanistic worldview, man is the result of his environment. The physical environment is the cause, and man's behavior is the effect. We see this in the theory of evolution and in the psychological theory of behaviorism (see lesson 6).

On the other hand, the biblical worldview sees the spiritual as the cause of the physical. By speaking God created the world out of nothing. History is the record of God fulfilling his purposes in time mainly through inspiring men to act. Biblically speaking causality begins with the invisible, not the physical.

Increasingly, physical causality is being used to excuse man's sinful behavior. Alcoholism is called a disease. Homosexuality is no longer considered a choice in behavior, but rather an uncontrollable predisposition determined by genetics and hormones. Children's behavior is commonly explained in terms of physical causality. Hyperactivity, for example, is often explained as a result of a diet of too much sugar.

Human nature's tendency toward irresponsibility is a main factor in this trend. If the cause of a child's undesirable behavior can be determined as something physical, then no one is responsible. Neither the child, nor his parents, nor his teachers can be blamed. And if a medical prescription seems to quell the symptoms, everybody is happy.

No one in his right mind would deny the connection between behavior, emotions, and physical changes and conditions in our bodies. Heart rate and blood pressure change when a person is angry or fearful. Body chemistry is greatly affected in times of stress. Medical technology is increasingly able to measure and monitor factors like brain waves and other

---

[47] Ibid., 30-31.

physical conditions in our bodies and correlate them with patterns of behavior. There is no doubt that certain physical conditions appear with certain behavioral patterns. The simultaneous occurrence of certain behaviors with certain physical conditions, however, does not indicate causality.

We do have scientific evidence that certain conditions like Downs Syndrome are the result of a genetic abnormality, but there is no scientific evidence that proves human choices of behavior are determined by physical causes. The modern trend to interpret human behavior in terms a physical causality is based on presupposition not scientific proof.

The problem is that today we tend to interpret practically all-human behavior in terms of physical causes. Too often we take the easy road of blaming the undesirable behavior of children on physical causes when we should be examining our parenting and teaching practices or raising our expectations of our children's behavior.

This brings us to the controversial and touchy subject of "learning disabilities." Today we have an epidemic of "learning disabilities" that include such "conditions" as attention deficit disorder and dyslexia. Although some physical conditions such as poor eyesight may be factors, we believe that many so-called "learning disabilities" are the result of poor parenting practices and poor teaching methods. We believe that systematic teaching methods, especially for teaching reading, can go a long way toward alleviating "learning disabilities."

For example, whole language advocates maintain that children learn to read in a "global fashion." They believe a child learns to read by coming to recognize whole words and groups of words in context, rather than learning the individual letters and letter combinations. According to whole language theory, a child gathers meaning from text through a variety of "cues" found in the text. Essentially the child is tackling reading a page at a time rather than a letter at a time. If dyslexia is the inability to see letters in their printed order, and if attention deficit disorder is an inability to focus, is there any better way to foster these "disabilities" than this "global fashion"?

The whole language contention that children learn to read "in a global fashion" is unsubstantiated. On the other hand, phonetic instruction encourages focus and concentration. The phonetic method of reading follows the text letter by letter in a linear fashion. Research shows that when we read, our eyes focus on one letter at a time.

Traditional systematic phonics concentrates on teaching very specific rules of the written language as isolated skills. Children are then taught how to reason from the general rule to the specific application. Every time a child applies a rule of phonics to a reading situation he is practicing deductive reasoning.

The whole language approach maintains that children do not need to be taught skills before they learn to read, but that they will learn them incidentally and randomly as they are reading. Whole language advocates claim that the practice of teaching the rules of phonics in isolation inhibits a child's ability to comprehend the text. They are wrong on this point too. Studies show that individual word recognition correlates highly with overall comprehension.

It is our opinion that much of today's epidemic of "learning disabilities," including dyslexia and attention deficit disorder, is caused by poor teaching methods. Furthermore, we believe that good teaching methods like systematic phonics are the best way to prevent "learning disabilities."

3. Teach math systematically and logically.

A Note about Teaching the Basics

What do employers wish their employees learned in school? What do college professors wish their students learned in high school? What do high school teachers wish their students learned in elementary school? What do upper elementary grade teachers wish their students learned in the primary grades? The answer to all these questions is basically the same. They wish their employees and students had a firm foundation in the "basics," the three R's, reading, writing, and 'rithmetic. Generally speaking these people are not overly concerned about how much knowledge of history, science, literature, or art their students and employees have. They want them to be able to read, write, add, and subtract.

If you are a primary grade teacher, you may feel that this whole burden is being unfairly thrown on your shoulders alone. You may feel you are already overloaded with expectations coming from all directions.

It is true, primary grade teachers are loaded down with expectations coming from all directions, but many of these expectations are misguided.

For example, there is the parental expectation that their children should have lots of fun in their first years of schooling. Christian parents are not much different from non-believers when it comes to expecting their teachers to entertain their children. Note that we are not advocating drudgery, but we believe that enjoyment of accomplishment and learning should provide satisfaction for the child, not the clever entertaining style of the primary grade teacher.

Then there are expectations that come from the humanistic philosophy of education. Among these are the socialization of the child, multicultural awareness, development of the "whole child" that includes subjects like health, physical education, and "life experiences" such as a field trip to the farm. Again, even though the parents are Christians, chances are they have accepted much of the humanistic philosophy of education.

On top of this are the expectations that come from the parental pride. Parents like to see tangible signs of their children's achievement. So primary teachers are expected to send home art projects, plan Christmas musical presentations, and organize science fairs.

We agree; primary grade teachers are overloaded with expectations. This is where headmasters, principals, school boards, and pastors need to intervene. Of course this means that they must have a firm grasp of the biblical worldview of education themselves. Then they need to begin the process of re-educating parents as to what are appropriate expectations for true biblical education. We have already addressed the issue of teacher as entertainer. (See lesson 8).

What about education of the "whole child"? Education of the "whole child" is a humanistic concept. Essentially this is an issue of jurisdiction. Under domination of the humanistic worldview, public schools have increasingly taken responsibility over children that properly belongs to the family. This has been an easy process since modern American parents have been all too willing to turn over to the schools' responsibilities that require their personal time and attention. Health, or personal hygiene, is an example. Who should be taking the time to tell children to brush their teeth, the school or parents? And when schools take time to teach these things, how much time is left to teach reading, writing, and arithmetic?

If we want primary grade teachers to concentrate on the three R's, we need to unload many of the unnecessary expectations they now labor under. Principals, school boards, and pastors must clarify priorities, first in their own minds, then with the school faculty, and then communicate this to the parents. This will not happen overnight, but with strong leadership, attitudes can be changed in time.

We are not advocating a sterile, Spartan-like atmosphere in the primary classroom. Music, history, and art are important. Knowledge of the Bible is essential. Again, we are calling for an adjustment in priorities, not the elimination of a rich and rounded educational experience. We must return to making the three R's our priority, and that will mean the elimination and reduction of other pursuits that take time away from this priority.

New Math

Some of you may remember the "new math" fiasco of the 1960's. If not, you may be familiar with the "new, new math" of the 1990's. Just as with the teaching of reading, there is an anti-traditional movement in the teaching of math. Humanistic educators have been trying for years to replace common sense in math with humanistic methods.

The new math of the 1990's is especially detrimental to a child's education. A number of humanistic themes enter in this latest fad. Among them is the humanistic preoccupation with the socialization of the child which advocates teaching math by cooperative group learning experiences. The humanistic fixation on "learning by discovery" has disparaged the teaching of math systematically, and their preference for kinesthetic learning has made the use of little wooden cubes and plastic bars of various lengths a lucrative business for the education industry along with the sale of calculators. The "learning by discovery" approach to math and collaborative learning approach (solving math problems by committee) are very unsystematic and extremely wasteful of classroom time.

The traditional approach to teaching math is deductive for the child, not inductive as the new math discovery approach advocates. Traditionally a child is given the rules of math and is taught how to use them. His reasoning process proceeds from the universal principle to the particular application. This does not mean that a teacher should not explain the reasons behind the rules. The humanistic criticism that many traditionalists teach rules without giving the reasons is accurate, though exaggerated. Elementary teachers need to understand basic math principles and impart this understanding to their students.

Math is a discipline that has its principles. Just as in teaching reading, teachers should teach these principles to the child in order to give him the tools of mastery over the subject. This is teaching math systematically

4. Require memorization.

During the twentieth century many American parents began to take a "hands off" approach to the religious training of their children. They claimed they did not want to "force religion on their children" because they wanted their children to be able to freely choose what they wanted to believe about God. Even Christian parents feared that imposing their religious beliefs on their children might make them into "phony Christians" who merely followed Christian practices because of parental pressure. This thinking comes from a humanistic worldview and would have been considered irresponsible parenting by previous generations. One of the results of this attitude was a reluctance to require that children memorize Bible verses.

Again, we can point to Dewey's influence on this issue also. The anti-traditional education biased stereotype has portrayed traditional teaching methods as heavy on tedious rote memorization of irrelevant facts by bored children. Whereas this may have been true in some cases, it certainly does not justify eliminating memorization as a legitimate part of a child's education. This humanist trend has gone to the extreme and done great harm to American education.

The Bible itself encourages memorization. Deuteronomy speaks of surrounding a child with the Word of God.

"Hear, O Israel: The Lord our God is one Lord: And thou shalt love the LORD thy God with all thine heart, and with all thy soul, and with all thy might. And these words, which I command thee this day, shall be in thine heart: And thou shalt teach them diligently unto thy children, and shalt talk of them when thou sittest in thine house, and when thou walkest by the way, and when thou liest down, and when thou risest up. And thou shalt bind them for a sign upon thine hand, and they shall be as frontlets between thine eyes. And thou shalt write them upon the posts of thy house, and on thy gates"
(Deuteronomy 6:4-9).

This passage flies in the face of the "hands off" approach to the religious upbringing of children. Adults are admonished to meditate on the scriptures. See Joshua 1:8. Meditation implies foreknowledge and familiarity. The word meditate comes from the same root as the word ruminate which refers to a cow chewing its cud. Several places in the Bible refer to keeping the Word of God in our hearts. See Psalms 40:8, Psalms 119:80, and Proverbs 3:3. This implies memorization. Even the phrase, "learn it by heart," means to memorize.

Contrary to humanistic psychology, it is not harmful to a child's self-esteem to require him to memorize. Nor does memorization damage a child's ability to comprehend. These are false beliefs that come from a humanistic philosophy of education. As a matter of fact, comprehension cannot even take place until there is knowledge in the mind to work with. Even Bloom's taxonomy acknowledges that taking in information is foundational in the ranking of thinking skills.

Bloom's Taxonomy of Thinking Skills

evaluation

synthesis

analysis

----

application

comprehension

information

In this taxonomy, the higher order thinking skills depend upon prior exercise of the lower skills. There can be no comprehension (understanding) until there is information (knowledge) in the child's mind first. This is one of the major problems with the humanist infatuation with process. There can be no mental process without content (knowledge) to work with.

It is obvious that children do not understand some or even much of what they memorize. This is not a reason to avoid memorization. Even adults carry knowledge in their memories that they do not totally comprehend. Some things, like the Word of God, will never be totally understood. To retain knowledge before it is understood is not harmful, especially to a child. Children are created with a capacity to memorize and even show a desire to memorize.

In the Bible, the Word of God is compared to seed (see Matthew 13). Seed remains dormant until the right conditions exist. Many Christian believers report their born-again experience as one of seeing familiar scripture suddenly come alive with personal meaning. Many of them had memorized these verses as small children. Thank God that their parents did not take the "hands off" approach to raising children.

Our discussion about memorization is not only true about scripture; it is true for many areas of study. The alphabet, the rules of phonics, and the multiplication tables are just a few examples. Children should be taught the reasons behind what they memorize in order to give them as much understanding as possible, but in many cases they are not going to have immediate comprehension. This should not prevent us from requiring memorization.

5.   Prioritize reading.

The argument for prioritizing reading runs much along the same line as our previous discussion in "A Note about Teaching the Basics." Teaching a child to read is the number one academic priority of the primary grades. Former President Clinton's program to have every child reading by grade four is too low of a standard. Christian school children should be reading in grade one. If we must eliminate some of the other expectations on first grade teachers to accomplish this, then we must. Literacy is the foundation of practically all future learning. A good reader will much more likely become a self-educator. Poor readers are handicapped learners. The inability to read is our nation's real number one "learning disability."

Literacy and Christianity

As noted earlier, literacy and Christianity have a history of working together. Wherever Christianity has made an impact, literacy has risen. This was especially true during the Reformation which gave rise to numerous translations of the Bible into vernacular languages. The Puritans in early America saw the connection between literacy and Christianity when they passed the Old Deluder Law. Historically when the Bible gets into the hands of literate people, that people experiences liberty. The liberty a nation experiences depends upon its level of literacy. At the time of the American Revolution, colonial America had the highest literacy rate of any nation in history to date.

The opposite is also true. Oppressed people tend to be illiterate. It is no accident that humanistic educational philosophy downplays literacy. It started with Rousseau and continues in the humanist tradition through Dewey's influence down to the present day whole language approach. This is not to say that every proponent of whole language theory is personally and deliberately allied with Satan against Christianity. But in effect, those who support humanistic philosophies that downplay literacy do harm to the cause of Christianity and liberty while they foster conditions for oppression.

Even today, through missionary efforts like the Wycliff Bible translators, Christianity encourages and supports literacy. All over the world hundreds of people groups that had no written languages have been blessed with the gift of phonetic alphabets and written language through the tireless effort of these missionaries.

God arbitrarily chose to leave us His revealing word in writing. Learning to read is the only appropriate response.

Quality Reading

We think with concepts. We communicate concepts with words. Words are containers of knowledge. Every time we add a word to our vocabulary, we add a concept to our minds. The more a child reads, the more his vocabulary increases. An increase in reading ability expands the mind. Studies have shown a correlation between command of vocabulary and success in a person's career. Parents and teachers commonly verify that children who read more tend to have greater command of vocabulary and broader general knowledge than poor readers.

Increasing vocabulary and expanding the mind, however, will only happen if prudence is used in the choice of reading material. Teacher and parental guidance are necessary to ensure that reading material is of high quality and broad in its scope. A narrow diet of superficial romance or science fiction fantasy will not expand the mind.

Modern secular education has become very lax on this issue. The traditional concept of "the classics" maintains that there are certain quality literary works that speak universal truth that transcends time and place. Although we may argue as to which specific books should be considered as classics and which should not, the realization that some books are worthy of special consideration is compatible with the biblical view of education. Christians are to judge all things (1 Cor 2:15). Our criteria, of course, should be biblical principles.

In guiding our children's reading, we must consider the age and maturity of the child. However, shielding the child from all content that contains violence and sin is not following the example of the Bible. The Bible is full of accounts of both violence and sin. The story of David and Goliath does not end with a stone from a slingshot. David finishes the job by cutting off Goliath's head. Yet the Bible does not glorify violence, nor does it glorify sin. Modern Hollywood glorifies both violence and sin. This is the heart of the issue of evaluating all literature, art, and music. Does it glorify God and truth or does it glorify violence or sin or man? Literature, art, or music does not have to be centered on a religious theme to glorify God. A quality painting of a sunset glorifies God because appreciation of the creation gives honor to its Creator. Stories that are not of a religious nature can glorify God by affirming truth. Even stories of people doing bad things can glorify God by affirming truth.

Literary accounts of sin that tempt, as in an explicit description of a sexual act, do not glorify God. Literature or art that make sin attractive does not glorify God. Although the Bible contains numerous accounts of murder and adultery, these accounts are never an occasion of temptation. Once again, the Bible itself is our best example.

6. <u>Emphasize and enforce good grammar.</u>

Most of the rules of grammar for the English language are easily understood. At least ninety percent of the grammatical errors children and adults make are caused by lack of diligence, not by a lack of understanding. There are some rules of grammar that may be difficult to understand, and we recognize that young children learning to write will make mistakes because they are still in the process of learning the rules. But after the initial learning phase, mistakes in grammar are much more likely to be issues of character than they are of ability.

Grammar is mostly an issue of discipline. Modern culture and secular education have completely lost appreciation for discipline. If we want to develop sound reasoning skills in our children, we must train them to be disciplined thinkers. Our long-term goal is that they become self-disciplined thinkers, but to bring them to that point, we will have to teach them by example and external discipline. This means insisting on correct grammatical usage in all student written work.

This can be a real trial for many teachers, especially if they have not developed their own attitude of appreciation for the rules of grammar. Let's face it, some of us have a bad attitude toward grammar. It is a lot of work to enforce, and all the trends in modern education see grammar as threatening to creativity. There is tremendous pressure on teachers to forego enforcing good grammar because humanistic thinking tells us that rules and conventions will stifle a child's creativity. As with all humanistic thinking, this too is wrong. Eliminating the rules of grammar does not nurture a child's creativity. On the contrary, neglecting to teach and train a child in the use of grammar will cripple his ability to write creatively. The rules of grammar are a writer's best friend, not his enemy. Grammar organizes language and makes it usable. The rules of capitalization and punctuation are conventions, that is, they are agreed upon rules that make written language consistent. Grammar facilitates communication.

Furthermore, grammar is logical. Understanding subjects and predicates is not just something to know for the next test in English. It is valuable practice in logical thinking. Learning grammar is training in logic.

Grammar is systematic. Words represent concepts. Sentences represent thoughts. Grammar organizes words into sentences externally while the mind is organizing concepts into thoughts internally. When a child is required to organize words on paper according to the rules of grammar, he is submitting not only his pen and paper to positive discipline, he is also submitting his thinking process to positive discipline. There are few things teachers can do that are more conducive toward developing sound reasoning skills than insisting on good grammar.

7. Teach the difference between cause-to-effect relationships and mere associations.

Deductive and Inductive Reasoning

Madison Avenue does not want the general public to think logically. The advertising industry stakes everything on the belief that people will forego logic when they shop. Advertising is not based upon logic. It is based upon feeling. Advertisers do not want consumers to think. They want them to feel. Products are associated with various feelings of well-being that have no logical connection to the product.

These advertisers are using behavior modification. Behavior modification is not reasoning. It is reflex, not reflection. It is external in that it takes place outside of the mind. The process bypasses conscious reflection. The subject of behavior modification is not fully using his mental capacity while he allows himself to be manipulated.

In effect, advertisers treat consumers like Pavlov treated his dog. They want them to salivate because of an illogical association of two unrelated phenomena that have absolutely no cause-to-effect relationship. Their strategy usually works. Every year consumers spend billions of dollars chasing these feelings of well-being. America is rapidly becoming an illogical culture. But God believes in logic. Isaiah 1:18 calls us to reason.

What does it mean to be reasonable? The phrase, "be reasonable," like so many other terms and phrases in modern English, has practically lost its meaning. It used to mean "to respect the rules of logic." Today it can mean practically anything, and it usually means "agree with me."

According to Webster's 1828 dictionary, to reason is to deduce inferences from premises. We sometimes call this deductive reasoning. Deductive reasoning starts with given facts or truth. It is the process of reaching a logical conclusion about a particular situation when given a general principle assumed to be true. It involves traveling mentally from a universal to a particular while maintaining submission to the laws of logic. A classic example of deduction would start with a given like "dogs have four legs." If we are given this fact and the fact that Spot is a dog, we can deduce that Spot has four legs.

Inductive reasoning is the reverse process. It begins with the observation of many particulars and ends with a conclusion that we call a generalization. If many dogs are observed to have four legs, one might reason to a generalization that all dogs have four legs. The "scientific method" is a rigorous application of inductive reasoning. After observing dozens of dogs all having four legs, one might hypothesize that all dogs have four legs. The scientific method requires that hypotheses be tested in an attempt to insure there are no exceptions. Since the only way to guarantee that the generalization, "all dogs have four legs," is absolutely true would be to examine every dog that has ever lived, this conclusion as all conclusions from inductive reasoning must always be provisional. This means the generalization will be accepted as a working "law" of science until an exception disproves it.

The chart below illustrates and compares the two kinds of reasoning:

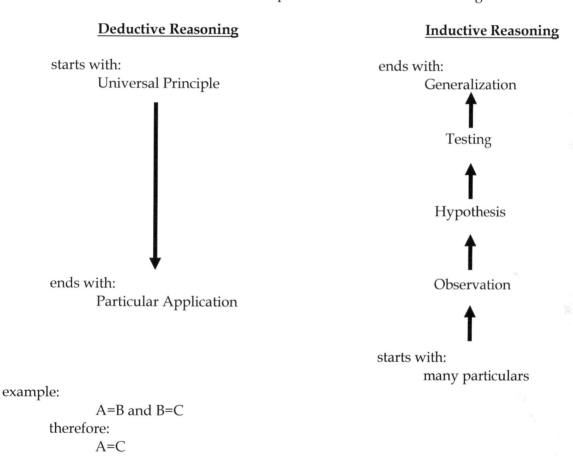

In deductive reasoning if the given is reliable, then the conclusion will be reliable. According to the Biblical worldview, the truth in the Bible is completely reliable. Biblical truth is more reliable than scientific "truth" because scientific "truth" is always subject to be proven false if and whenever contrary evidence is discovered. Biblical truth is unchanging and completely reliable. Since we live in a culture that practically worships scientific knowledge, it is important that teachers communicate this important difference between biblical truth and scientific knowledge to their students.

Reasoning is the process of traveling from cause to effect as in deductive reasoning, or from effect to cause as in inductive reasoning. When someone asks you the reason why you did something, you begin your answer with "because," and then you give your reason. "Because" is a shortening of the two words, "by" and "cause." Reasoning is the process of connecting cause with effect.

Modern American culture is abandoning reason. People prefer to go by their "gut feelings" and prejudices rather than take the effort to think things through. Our nation is becoming mentally lazy. Reason is work. It is a mental activity. Our culture increasingly prefers passivity.

As Christian educators we do not want our children to follow cultural trends, especially this one. We want our children to be competent thinkers able to see clearly the connection between cause and effect. Good teaching methods will go a long way toward giving our children that ability.

Reasoning Skill Comes by Training

One of the reasons Americans are abandoning reasoning is because they are no longer trained to reason in school. As mentioned earlier, the lack of a systematic approach in humanistic education with its child-centered classrooms, random learning, and its infatuation with "learning by discovery" has lead to chaotic thinking habits in children. Most graduates of today's public schools have never been exposed to good examples of sound reasoning.

One way to train children to reason effectively is with a formal class in logic. An increasing number of Christian schools are doing just that. But sound deductive reasoning should be taught from the child's first learning experiences in school. For young children teaching reading by using systematic phonics is excellent training in deductive reasoning. Children are given the rules (the universal) and trained to make application to specific situations (particulars). Every time a child applies a rule of phonics he is building sound mental habits.

The application of the rules of grammar is also excellent practice in deductive reasoning. Some teachers fail to appreciate the value of learning grammatical concepts like subjects, predicates, case, and when to use "who" and when to use "whom." It is possible that the majority of modern teachers have never even heard of diagramming sentences. Yet all these practices are very good training in deductive reasoning. Math, especially geometry, is also excellent training in reasoning skills.

We have abandoned the traditional concept of transferable skills. In past generations it was believed that learning a subject like Latin, especially Latin grammar, was good training in logical thinking. Being pragmatists, the humanists came along and said since Latin is a "dead language," it is of no use to the student in the "here and now" and therefore it should be abandoned.

The pragmatism in humanistic thinking has led to the modern trend to prefer "learning by discovery." This philosophy believes that the purpose of education is to serve man. Truth is not the goal of learning; problem solving is. The goal of learning by discovery is to find a way that, as the popular expression says, "works for me." Learning by discovery is basically trial and error. It is the method of Whole Language and the new, new math. It is an undisciplined approach that leaves the child helpless and ill-equipped to handle future intellectual challenges. It is not even a good example of inductive thinking.

Inductive reasoning is best taught in upper level science classes. As mentioned earlier, the scientific method is an example of inductive reasoning. Learning by discovery is not the scientific method. The scientific method requires strict control over the process. It is rigorous and disciplined. It is highly unlikely these conditions can be met in a classroom with younger children. Although science "experiments" are popular with elementary children and their parents, in general they tend to be an inefficient use of class time. Younger children can learn more science in less time by reading and observation.

In history and literature classes teachers can foster sound reasoning habits by fashioning their questions toward thinking rather than feeling. Frequently teacher's guides suggest questions asking how children feel about the subject under study. Other suggestions are toward encouraging children to express themselves intuitively. Teachers can correct this imbalance by using questions that relate to cause and effect.

This can be done by using essay questions on tests rather than multiple choice, true or false, or fill in the blank questions. As mentioned earlier, it is important that children learn information and facts, but children can learn facts by mere association. In essay questions the teacher can ask the important cause-to-effect question, "Why?"

Sound reasoning is more an issue of discipline than intelligence. The reasonable person is a person of self-discipline. He is able to focus on facts and rise above feeling and prejudice. Sound reasoning is not obtained by reading a book about sound reasoning. It requires concentrated, conscious reflection and control of the internal thought process. It is a habit that is developed by consistent training.

8. Teach with concepts (words) rather than images (pictures).

The Bible tends to be anti-image. One of the Ten Commandments says, *"Thou shalt not make unto thee any graven image, or any likeness of any thing that is in heaven above, or that is in the earth beneath, or that is in the water under the earth:"* (Exodus 20:4). The fact that the Bible itself is a book of words and not pictures indicates a preference. As a matter of fact, Jesus is the Word made flesh.

The world, on the other hand, is into images in a big way. According to tennis star, Andre Agassi, in a TV commercial for a camera company, "Image is everything!" He is right. Modern America is preoccupied with images. The pop music scene is all about images. Talent has very little to do with it anymore. The secret to success in pop music is to create a "cool" image and package it so it will sell concert tickets and recordings. Image is very important to modern Americans, especially the younger generation.

The Bible points out how foolish this is. Isaiah describes a man cutting down a tree and using part of the wood to make a fire to cook his food, and another part of the wood to carve an idol. *"And the residue thereof he maketh a god, even his graven image: he falleth down unto it, and worshippeth it, and prayeth unto it, and saith, Deliver me; for thou art my god* (Isaiah 44:17).

Isaiah is saying that men take ordinary wood, the same wood they burn in their cooking fires, and then they worship it. How smart can that be? It is just common wood, but they attribute superhuman power to it. Yet our modern culture does the exact same thing. Our formula is this. Take an ordinary person. Add an image, and you get a celebrity. Then we worship the celebrity. If the ancient Greeks could visit modern America, they would feel right at home religiously. The only difference would be that their Pantheon was in Athens, and ours is in Hollywood.

Our problem with images is not limited to the use of images with people. The use of images as media presents serious problems in communication and education as well. The trouble with images is that they are not exact. They are full of connotation, implication, and innuendo. They are open for subjective interpretation. The viewer of an image can give it his own meaning. Like the man mentioned in Isaiah who attributed supernatural meaning to a piece of wood, this can get us into trouble. Concepts are much more exact.

The chart below summarizes the difference between concepts and images:

Concept	Image
word	picture
universal	particular
abstract	concrete
essence (Hebrew-internal)	form (Greek-external)
cognitive (mental)	affective (emotional)
objective	subjective
unambiguous	ambiguous
(only one meaning)	(many possible meanings, connotation, implication, inference, innuendo)
active	passive
(requires mental engagement)	(mentally relaxed)
linear	non-linear
(left to right focus)	(wholesale encounter)
logical	illogical
(under authority of logic)	(outside rules of logic)

We represent concepts with words and images with pictures. These pictures can be still pictures or moving pictures as in video and movies.

A concept is universal and abstract. It can be used in a variety of situations. Consider the concept of hot or heat for example. It can be used in multiple situations. An image is particular and concrete. It is of a unique thing, event, or person. We cannot have an image of heat, but we can have an image of a hot sidewalk or a hot potato.

Concepts deal with essence. We studied the difference between the Hebrew (biblical) worldview and the Greek (humanistic) worldview earlier in this course. The Hebrews focused on the internal essence of things, especially God and men. The Greeks were preoccupied with external form. Images convey externals like form.

Concepts are cognitive. They are dealt with mentally. Images are affective. They affect our emotions. Concepts can leave us emotionally cold. Images stir emotional response, even if ever so slightly.

One of the most important distinctions between concepts and images is that concepts are objective while images tend to be subjective. Concepts have commonly accepted meaning. The meaning of a concept remains constant. Images, on the other hand, can be interpreted subjectively. Different individuals viewing the same image can come away with entirely different impressions. Images are ambiguous. They can convey a message indirectly by connotation, implication, inference, and innuendo, whereas the single meaning in a concept is conveyed directly without any secondary message.

When a concept is encountered, active mental engagement is required. Images are encountered from a mentally relaxed posture. When words are read from a page, the eyes and mind of the reader must focus on the written letters in a linear left to right progression. On the other hand, images, are viewed wholesale. No focus is required. When concepts are strung

105

together into complete thoughts they are governed by the rules of logic. Images obey no rules of logic.

The point is not that images have no value in education. Video, for example, can be a tremendous aid in the classroom. Viewing videos on science and nature and geographic videos of distant lands and interesting peoples can greatly enhance teaching subjects like science and geography.

Nor does our discussion on images and the Bible mean we should eliminate art from the Christian school curriculum.

The problem is the over use of images in the teaching process, especially when you consider the fact that the average child today spends an incredible amount of time each week in front of the television. The amount of time he spends watching television and playing video games is several times what he spends reading. Most of us forget that this is a relatively new phenomenon. Before the coming of television (around 1950), reading was the only option a child had. In a single generation America changed from mainly a print media culture to an image media culture. The implications of this revolution are tremendous, but hardly noticed by the average American. For excellent insight into this subject read Neil Postman's book, *Amusing Ourselves to Death*.

The over use of image media damages and destroys the development of sound reasoning skills. Viewing video is a mentally passive experience. Children are much more likely to be mentally passive in their out of school time. Statistics show that they are not likely to choose activities that will develop sound reasoning skills on their own. This is all the more reason why Christian schools must be very deliberate in choosing methods that will foster the development of sound reasoning skills in their students.

9. Instill a love for truth.

Jesus said, *"I am the Way, the Truth, and the Life"* (John 14:6). In Matthew 22:37 we are commanded to *"love the Lord thy God with all thy heart, and with all thy soul, and with all thy mind."* The equation is simple. We are commanded to love God. God is truth. Therefore, we are to love truth.

God determines all truth. Truth is defined by God. If something agrees with God, it is true. If it disagrees with God, it is false.

But some would say there are two kinds of truth, Truth with a capital "T" and truth with a small "t." They would say Truth refers to the things about God, like the fact that Jesus is God. They would say capital "T" truth is found in the Bible while small "t" truth is found in other places like in the testimony of a witness in court.

This dichotomy is misleading. Truth is a quality. Truth is not plural. There is no "what is true for you may not be true for me" and "what is true for me may not be true for you." To say this is a perversion of the use of the word, truth. Ultimate Truth and truth are not two, but one. Truth is a quality of God. It is found first in the Bible, but it is also found in God's creation.

Francis Bacon said that God has given us two books of revelation, creation which theologians call general revelation, and the Bible which theologians call special revelation. In Romans chapter one Paul says that men ought to see the truth about God by looking at His creation, but they don't because of their own sin. *"Because that which may be known of God is manifest in them; for God hath showed it unto them. For the invisible things of him from the creation of the world are clearly seen, being understood by the things that are made, even his eternal power and*

Godhead; so that they are without excuse: "(Romans 1:19-20). Sin has corrupted men's ability to read the book of God's creation.

In his mercy, God has given us a second chance in His special revelation, the Bible. Receiving the truth of the Bible is not dependent upon man's intellectual ability. Truth from the Bible comes by faith. Understanding comes after faith. Whereas man, through his own sin, destroyed his ability to know truth through his own intellectual striving, through God's grace he is able to know truth by merely trusting in the special revelation found in the Bible.

But the blessing of special revelation does not end with knowing the truth about God. The Bible gives us the keys to understanding his creation. In Lesson 1 we called this the advantage of revelation. Special revelation restores man's ability to see truth in creation.

The word, "truth," has been abused. Humanistic man has corrupted it for his own selfish purposes. We must return to an attitude of awe and respect for truth. As teachers we must model this attitude in our words and actions.

To impart a love for truth we must first have it in our own hearts internally, and then we must express it externally. The outward expression of this attitude is not just a matter of how we treat the subject matter under study. The way we discipline our students will reveal our attitude toward truth. If we sacrifice truth for expediency, the children in our care will be affected.

Consider this example. The class mascot (teddy bear) is missing from its place on the top of the bookshelf. The teacher approaches the issue pragmatically and says, "If the person who took Teddy does not return him to his place by lunch time, the whole class will be deprived of afternoon recess." What is wrong with this approach? Truth is sacrificed for the sake of a return to order. Children will get a message that external peace is more important than truth and justice. Their little minds want to know the truth about who took Teddy. They desire accountability and justice. Every time decisions are made for the sake of expediency at the cost of truth and justice, a little more of the desire for truth dies inside a child and a little more cynicism is planted in his heart.

This is the plea bargain mentality. A teacher should never plea-bargain with her class. Children want to know if truth and justice really count with their teacher. Do you know God does not agree with the plea-bargaining mentality? There will be no plea bargains on Judgment Day.

Our goal should be to make students into seekers of truth. We want to instill in our students a desire to know the truth about everything they study. We don't want them to just know what Aristotle, or Thomas Jefferson, or Mark Twain said; we want them to have a desire to know if what these men said is true or not.

This is real critical thinking. It is evaluation---the top item on Bloom's taxonomy. The big difference between the humanistic view of evaluation and the biblical view centers on the criteria used to evaluate. For the humanist, man is his own criteria. Humanistically thinking, man's opinion is the judge. For the Christian, God's word is the judge.

Humanistic education is preoccupied with encouraging even very young children to form opinions about everything. Secular education believes that children need to feel their opinion is important in order to develop positive self-esteem. This is one area where humanistic education has been a smashing success. The average American today feels very good about his own opinions.

As Christian educators we want our students to value God's opinion, not their own. We want them to take on the attitude of Christ. Jesus never began a statement with "In my opinion," "I think," or "I feel." Most often He began with "It is written." Jesus was not interested in forming His own opinions. His Father's opinion was good enough. His Father's opinion is truth and Jesus is a lover of truth.

We must be careful that we do not give children the impression that truth is found within themselves. One of the mottos of modern man is, "Be true to yourself." This comes from the false belief that truth is found inside a person. This thinking comes from the Hindu and Buddhist worldview and has been popularized by Hollywood in movies like the Star Wars series where the heroes listen to the "truth" of the "Force" within them.

It may be humbling to recognize that truth does not come from our own original thinking, but it's the truth. We can nurture the attitude of respect for truth in our students by the kind of questions we ask them. We can begin fewer of our questions with "How do you feel?" or "What is your opinion?" and we can ask more questions like "Is it true?"

Along with teaching children respect for truth comes teaching them respect for authority. Generally speaking, Christian educators teach their students respect for authority figures like parents, teachers, pastors, the police, etc. Hopefully they are also teaching their students respect in some of the older Christian traditions that our humanistic culture has eliminated. Some of these are respect for age, special respect for women and girls, respect for the Lord's Day, and even respect for places of worship.

When it comes to fostering a love for truth, there are other kinds of respect we need to impart to our students. Every human opinion is not as good as every other human opinion, and we need to teach our children to respect the authority of wisdom, experience, knowledge, and expertise.

In the same vein, our students need to develop a respect for the authority of primary sources and eyewitnesses. One way we can do this, of course, is to use primary sources more often and speak of them with respect. Perhaps a teacher could keep a copy of the Declaration of Independence in a place of honor in her classroom.

One of the more important authorities we should teach our children to respect is the authority of fact. By asking for factual support of statements and theories proposed by students, teachers can impress upon them the importance of getting the facts. Contemporary Americans no longer care to know the facts. They are enamored with their own opinions. This is extreme foolishness. *"Professing themselves to be wise, they became fools,"* (Romans 1:22) Because of this attitude our culture is losing touch with reality. *"And even as they did not like to retain God in their knowledge, God gave them over to a reprobate mind, to do those things which are not convenient;"* (Romans 1:28). A culture that no longer cares about facts is bound for destruction.

Real seekers of truth will desire factual knowledge. They will stay in touch with reality. They will be the hope for the future of our civilization. By nurturing a love for truth in their students, Christian educators can make an impact far beyond the walls of their classrooms.

10. Demand attentiveness and diligence.

Aptitude is a reality. The emphasis in this lesson has been on the connection between reasoning and discipline. The fact is that some individuals find mathematical reasoning easy while others do not. Some individuals find creative writing and the fine arts easy while others do not. Praise God for individual differences. Diversity gives glory to the Creator.

But there is an aspect of life where one size fits all. This is the area of morality. One set of commandments does fit all. Regardless of an individual's aptitudes, personality type, or past history, "Thou shalt not kill" and all of God's commandments apply equally to all. There is only one standard for Christian character, and it does not bend for personality or aptitude differences.

Christian schools pride themselves on making character a priority. Whereas the public school system has retreated from the arena of developing strong character in their students, Christian schools work hard at it.

Humanistic influence, however, has confused even some of the best-intentioned Christian educators. Even though they are committed to developing strong Christian character in their students, many Christian educators have confused issues of ability with issues of character. In many Christian schools where dishonesty, immodesty, and disrespect would never be tolerated, lack of diligence is accepted. This strange inconsistency often goes undetected by both parents and educators because humanistic attitudes and stereotypes about traditional education continue to prevail.

Diligence is not an issue of intelligence or ability. It may be true that some individuals have an aptitude for neater penmanship than others, but a discerning teacher can determine when a child is being diligent or not. Diligence is a character issue. We are doing our students a great disservice if we demand some forms of Christian behavior but tolerate lack of diligence.

The same is true for attentiveness. While it is true that some children will have a more difficult time with paying attention to their teacher than others, there is a reasonable standard that all children can be expected to meet. One of the main reasons attentiveness has become a problem in today's classrooms is because of low expectancy from parents and teachers. Attentiveness is basically a character issue.

Individual differences are never an excuse for sin. Some people have more trouble resisting alcohol abuse than others. Drunkenness is still a sin. Although some people may struggle with it more than others, self-control is still a virtue. Attentiveness and diligence are forms of self-control. Strong character comes more by training than by teaching. It is the consistent, persistent hard work of parents and teachers that develops diligence and attentiveness in children.

This is obviously not an easy task. The battle is not just against the fallen human nature in our children, it is against erroneous thinking that prevails in the minds of Christians themselves. But the fruit of our labor will be sweet. Children who are diligent and attentive will become clearer thinkers. They will develop sound reasoning skills. They will emerge as the leaders of our church and our nation.

Summary

To some readers this lesson may sound like a call to a strict Spartan-like lifestyle that has no appreciation for the sensitive, intuitive side of life. They may think that we are advocating only one side of the left-brain, right-brain debate. It may even seem to some that we have no appreciation for the humanities and the fine arts because of our emphasis on analytical thinking. Others may even see us as "sexist" because we emphasize traits more commonly identified as more natural to the masculine temperament than the feminine temperament.

If we lived in ancient Sparta perhaps we would be advocating a return to the intuitive, sensitive, "feminine" qualities. But we live in modern America. We need to understand the times. We must be like the tiny tribe of Issachar. *"And of the children of Issachar, which were men that had understanding of the times, to know what Israel ought to do;"* (1 Chronicles 12:32).

We think art, music, the humanities, and intuitive sensitivity are all very important. Nothing in this course should be taken as a devaluation of these things. But we live in a time when reasoning is being neglected. As a culture we are way out of balance. This may not be easy to see because we are immersed in the culture. But when we rise above our cultural environment and view the issue from a historical perspective, we can see how far contemporary

America has strayed from the standards of past centuries. And when we look at the unchanging standards in God's Word, we get the objectivity that enables us to understand the times.

Lesson 10

The Restoration of Biblical Education

Goals:

1. To gain a deeper appreciation of the Christian school movement and the Christian home school movement.
2. To gain insight into how the Christian school movement and Christian home school movement can become a more effective tool for God's purposes.

Assignment:

1. Read Lesson 10.
2. Write answers to Study Questions below.

Study Questions:

1. Why are Christian schools and Christian home schools the only hope for the restoration of American education?
2. How was the first phase of the Christian school movement the beginning of the restoration of American education?
3. Why is the view that academic excellence and sound biblical doctrine come from two separate sources wrong? How has this attitude hindered the development of Christian education?
4. How can Christian textbooks hinder the development of the biblical worldview?

For Further Study (see resource list):

Rose, James B. *A Guide to American Christian Education for the Home and School: The Principal Approach*

Wilson, Douglas. *Recovering the Lost Tools of Learning.* Wheaton, IL: Crossway Books, 1991.

Lesson 10

The Restoration of Biblical Education

"Behold, I set before you this day a blessing and a curse; A blessing, if ye obey the commandments of the Lord your God, which I command you this day: And a curse, if ye will not obey the commandments of the Lord your God, but turn aside out of the way which I command you this day, to go after other gods, which ye have not known."
    (Deut. 11:26-28)

Modern American education is under a curse. We have previously referred to this curse as "the dumbing down of America." As reiterated throughout this course, differences in our views of how to educate are rooted in our worldview, and worldview is at root a spiritual issue. America has turned its back on God, and we are reaping the bad fruit.

The only hope for the restoration of American education is the Christian school movement and the Christian home school movement. But these movements themselves are subject to error. Only to the degree that these movements stay true to the biblical worldview, and only to the degree that the individuals involved in these movements maintain their own personal integrity, will these movements succeed.

The focus of this course is on worldview and the philosophical basis of our practices in education. It is extremely important, however, to realize that personal integrity and spiritual maturity are absolutely necessary. All the correct thinking in the world will do you no good if you do not have the character to put your worldview into your everyday practice. Putting the biblical worldview into practice is not easy. God's ways are not the slacker's ways. Consistency and perseverance are essential. Christian educators must be leaders as defined by Jesus himself. That is, we must be self-sacrificing servants. We must find our reward where Jesus did. *"Jesus saith unto them, My meat is to do the will of him that sent me, and to finish his work."* (Jn 4:34)

As Christian educators we have a heavy responsibility. We are placed in positions of great importance and we need to take heed of the scripture that says, *"My brethren, be not many masters (teachers), knowing that we shall receive the greater condemnation."* (James 3:1)

But along with the responsibility comes the opportunity to be a part of a glorious work, the restoration of biblical education. By no means are we attempting to predict the future of American education. The outcome is in the hands of the Lord. And our goal is not to prop up any human civilization. We were created to glorify God. Falsehoods do not glorify God. Education that reflects the truth of the Bible glorifies God. A generation of Christians educated from a biblical worldview will glorify God. And a generation of Christians educated from a biblical worldview can restore not only American education, but the nation and culture as a whole.

The Christian School Movement

Some Christian denominations have maintained a strong emphasis on Christian education throughout the centuries, but as we noted earlier, the majority of American Christians have come to depend on state controlled humanistic public education. Nineteenth and early twentieth century public schools may not have seemed so humanistic and hostile toward Christianity, but by the middle of the twentieth century many Christian parents began to wake up to the fact that public education was harmful to their children. This gave birth to the modern Christian school movement.

The first phase of the modern Christian school movement began in the 1960's and 1970's after the U.S. Supreme Court had issued decisions that threw out prayer and the Bible from public education. It can be characterized by the following:

The Christian School Movement

<u>First phase (1960's and 1970's)</u>

- Parent led
- Christian teachers
- Bible added to secular textbooks
- No large Christian textbook publishers
- Beginning of restoration of biblical jurisdiction

It is important to note that the Christian school movement was started by parents and not by Christian teachers. If we define "Christian teachers" as teachers who teach in Christian schools, the reason why that group did not lead the modern movement is obvious. In the early 1960's there were very few Christian teachers in Christian schools and they were already committed to Christian schools in their denominations.

But if we define "Christian teachers" as Christians who teach in public schools, there were certainly enough of them to start of a movement. The impetus for the movement did not come from them, however. It appears that they themselves, like most American Christians, had come under the influence of humanism to the degree that they saw no conflict between public education and Christianity.

A small percentage of Christian parents did, however, conclude that the public schools were no longer the place for their own children. Some pastors caught the vision to start Christian schools in their churches, but most of the Christian schools in the early phase of the movement were started by small groups of parents. For the most part they had little or no financial assistance from local churches. As a result, they often started small and with many parent volunteers serving as teachers. Although many of these "teachers" were not professionally trained as educators, they were dedicated Christians. A new priority was established that made the teacher's faith more important than their professional training.

There were no large Christian publishers of textbooks at the beginning of the modern Christian school movement. Most of the start up schools merely added the Bible to the secular textbooks available. Gradually publishers of Christian educational materials appeared.

Some of these earlier publishers came out with materials that were geared to small schools that had only a few children at any one grade level. These materials often took the form of booklets that were intended for self-instruction. Parents would act as monitors while children of different ages completed booklet after booklet at their own pace.

The important thing about this early phase was that Christian parents began to take back their biblical responsibility to educate their children. This was the beginning of the restoration of the biblical jurisdiction of education.

The Christian School Movement

<u>Second phase (1970's to the early 1980's)</u>

- Led by Christian educators
- Christian publishers of textbooks
- Beginning of restoration of biblical content

By this second phase of the Christian school movement, schools were growing large enough to hire full time teachers. Many of these teachers had experience in public schools. Paid administrators and principals could now be full time in many Christian schools. School boards were established. Regional, national, and international Christian school associations appeared. In time, the leadership of Christian schools passed out from under the direct control of parents to the control of full time, paid Christian educators. By this we do not imply that Christian parents lost control of Christian schools. Christian schools certainly are much more accountable to parents than public schools where accountability to parents and local control have virtually disappeared. But relative to the earlier phase of the movement, a new group of professional Christian educators began to take over leadership of the Christian school movement. This has both its advantages and its pitfalls.

One of the advantages of full time paid Christian educators is that they can dedicate full time and attention to the improvement of Christian education. Coming together in associations with other Christian schools has enabled them to share insights and glean wisdom from each other. Being paid and full time has enabled many Christian schoolteachers to further their own education by attending seminars and taking courses at Christian colleges. There are many other advantages that come from a system of paid full time "professionals."

However, it is in this concept of "professional" that also lie some potential pitfalls. We have already discussed the "education industry" that exists in secular education. The modern secular education industry with its billions of dollars in payroll to millions of teachers, administrators, college professors, book publishers, politicians, and teachers' unions has become a self-serving monster that tyrannizes American education. It no longer serves, but demands to be served.

If there is a Christian education industry, it certainly does not approach the scale of the secular industry. But the pitfalls of "professionalism" come with the status. American history is full of accounts of Christian ministries that have degenerated into self-serving institutions. If we are not vigilant, our fate will be the same. Our attitude must be one of constant self-scrutiny and openness to criticism from within and without.

Christian "Professionals"

Most American Christians today are influenced by an anti-intellectual attitude that sees academic excellence and sound biblical doctrine as coming from two distinctly separate sources. Parents often want Christian education that is both biblically sound and academically excellent. The assumption is that the experts on the Bible know nothing about academics, and the experts in academics know nothing about the Bible. Unfortunately, these assumptions may be more accurate today, but throughout most of the history of Christianity, academic excellence and knowledge of and reverence for the Bible came from the same source. The separation of biblical faith and academic excellence is a modern concept. It is the result of over a century of anti-intellectualism in the evangelical Church. Christians have retreated from intellectual pursuit and humanism has taken over academia.

This explains why Christian colleges want PhDs on their faculties. The public mentality is that you must add academic knowledge to sound biblical doctrine to get quality Christian education. This mentality trickles down to Christian elementary and high schools. Christians want "professionally prepared" teachers. They even demand state certified teachers as some sort of guarantee that they will be "professionally prepared." This is a major pitfall.

Today the humanists virtually own academia. They determine the worldview that governs acceptable academic pursuit. They set the rules and they confer degrees on those who submit to their rules. Herein lies a huge problem. To get academic credentials, one must submit himself to a barrage of humanistic propaganda. It is very difficult to remain unaffected by this onslaught of the humanist worldview. This of course varies with the area of study. For example, the study of math and science in today's universities tend to be less influenced by humanistic thought than study of history, literature, the "social sciences," and education. Also degrees from Christian institutions can be less influenced by humanistic thought, though unfortunately this is often not the case. Generally speaking, getting a college degree in America today means indoctrination in the humanist worldview.

As noted earlier, some astute Christian writers consider 1805 a key date in American history because it marks the transition of control of academic leadership (in this case Harvard College) from the hands of orthodox Christians to the humanistic Unitarians. From that date forward humanism progressively gained control over American academia until today's total domination. So what is the solution? Do we retreat further into our Christian ghetto? Do we allow anti-intellectualism to grow even stronger in the evangelical church? Has the Church become intellectually bankrupt?

We believe it is the secular culture, not the Church, that is intellectually bankrupt. Intellectual pursuit controlled by a humanistic worldview, because it rejects revelation, is doomed. The logical consequence of the current direction of American academia is intellectual decadence that will lead our civilization into a new Dark Age. The only hope for our civilization is the revival of the biblical worldview as the guiding light of academic pursuit, and the vehicle for the injection of the biblical worldview into intellectual pursuit is Christian education.

Good teachers from a biblical perspective are quite different from "professionally prepared" teachers from the world's perspective. Christians must abandon the world's standards of educational professionalism and adopt biblical standards. Rather than BAs, MAs, and PhDs, we need to value intellectual leadership that is rooted in the biblical worldview. Rather than state certification for teachers, which merely means they have submitted to indoctrination in the humanistic doctrines of "tolerance," multiculturalism, and the feminist and homosexual agendas, we need Christian school association certification that prioritizes knowledge of the biblical worldview as an essential qualification to teach in a Christian school.

New wine requires new wineskins. Much of the spiritual and intellectual leadership in the Church today is coming from newer sources. Many of the traditional sources of leadership have become compromised institutions whose top priority is self-promotion or self-preservation. Newer, leaner, more in tune with the Holy Spirit ministries are springing up in the Church. We encourage you to become familiar with many of these new ministries. Many of them are small and Internet based. Please refer to the "resources" section of this manual for the names of some of these ministries. This would not be the first time in history for God to choose to do a great and mighty work through humble beginnings.

The potential impact of Bible-based Christian education on the Church and on our culture is immense. If humanism remains in control, it is just a matter of time before public education will collapse. The intellectual bankruptcy of humanism will create a nation aching for intellectual leadership. If we do our job, our graduates will be prepared to assume that leadership. Christian colleges and universities would once again become the seat of our nation's spiritual and intellectual leadership.

Christian Textbooks

During the 1970's, Christian schools in the U.S. started at the rate of one a day. Soon the demand for Christian textbooks made it possible for publishers to operate on a profitable scale and larger companies like A Beka Books and Bob Jones University Press became the main suppliers of textbooks to the Christian school movement. These new Christian textbooks eliminated many of the humanistic errors in the secular textbooks, but they were far from perfect. We are certainly grateful for the many improvements these publishers have made over secular textbooks, and we are grateful for the efforts made to continue to improve them. But the influence of humanism runs deep, and much humanistic influence still infects even the textbooks produced by well meaning Christian publishers.

Part of the problem is the failure to examine assumptions that underlie the structure and content of modern American education. Humanistic assumptions creep into the Christian textbooks. For example, one elementary level history book states that, "History is the story of people and the things they have done." This may seem like a relatively harmless statement, and it may be the unexamined assumption of the majority of adult Christians today, but it is a false statement according to the biblical worldview. According to the Bible, history is the story of God fulfilling his purposes in time. This biblical view of history reflects the essential Christian doctrine of the sovereignty of God. Before humanism gained dominant influence in America, Christians believed in providential history. They saw all events controlled by God who is the focal point and the beginning and end of all history. Statements like the one quoted from this Christian textbook are not harmless. They are part of a process of indoctrination into a humanistic worldview.

The choice of what content to include in textbooks is also controlled by worldview. Modern secular textbooks have excluded much content that is threatening to the humanist worldview and replaced it with emphasis that supposedly supports the humanist worldview. Unfortunately, many Christian textbooks, like the one previously sited, follow the content selection pattern of the secular books. For example, this same textbook fails to mention evangelism as part of Columbus' motivation for sailing to the New World. This same book unwittingly follows the multiculturalism agenda by dedicating large portions of text to the Native Americans, emphasizing the positive qualities of their cultures while failing to mention the depravities of their pagan cultures. There are only so many pages between the covers of a textbook. Decisions have to be made as to what to include or exclude. The humanists have effectively censored Christianity from their textbooks and replaced it with propaganda to further their agenda. Christian publishers must not allow the humanist patterns to influence their selection of content.

Christian publishers should be credited for starting the restoration of biblical content to American education. Their shortcomings, however, are serious and need immediate correction.

The Christian School Movement

<u>Third phase (mid-1980's to the present)</u>

- Realization that Christian teachers and Christian books are not enough
- Growing understanding of the worldview issue
- Beginning of restoration of biblical methods

By the mid-1980's the pace of the growth of the Christian school movement began to slow and the Christian home school movement got underway. There is a link between the two. Many of the early home schoolers came out of Christian schools. To some degree the start of the home school movement was due to discontent with existing Christian schools. The factors were multiple. Tuition cost was definitely one of them. School discipline and peer group problems were another. Many of the new home schoolers left the Christian schools because they felt the Christian schools were too similar to secular schools. It is to this group that we need to listen.

By the 1980's Christian schools had Christian teachers and Christian books, yet a growing number of parents were saying their Christian school was not Christian enough. Then in the early 1990's a new more widespread awareness of the importance of a Christian worldview gained attention in the church. Parents began to demand Christian education that would give their children a Christian worldview. Soon schools began to emphasize Christian worldview on their brochures and promotional material. Virtually all Christian schools promised education with a Christian worldview. Yet there was a growing awareness that this was indeed not the case.

Surveys showed that children from Christian homes were thinking more like their secular peers than the biblical worldview. Results from the biblical worldview tests conducted by the Nehemiah Institute showed that scores from students in Christian schools were actually declining. It became evident to many that Christian teachers and Christian textbooks were not enough.

This is where the Christian school movement stands today. The movement is at a crossroads. We can continue to pretend Christian education is winning the battle for the minds of our children, or we can take a good hard look at our own education philosophy and practice. We believe the hope for the future is with those Christian schools and home schooling families who are willing to submit all their thinking to biblical principle. This means being willing to relinquish all our pet presuppositions about education and allow the Bible to give us our philosophy of education. It means that our methods also must conform to biblical principle. Those schools that embrace this attitude have begun restoring biblical methods to the education process.

There is a bright spot in the results of the Nehemiah Institute's worldview testing. A minority of Christian schools have maintained very high scores on the PEERS test. These are schools that have taken special care to train their staff in the biblical worldview. They are schools that submit every facet of their educational process to biblical principle. They are the hope for the future of Christian education in America. We challenge you to join them.

117

C.E.U. Credit

Nehemiah Institute is an authorized C.E.U. provider for several Christian school associations including: ACSI/SCACS/AACS/FLOCS/ILOCS/FACE. Two C.E.U. credits are awarded with the following:

- Completion of this course, under supervised study
- Completion of PEERS Testing
- Essay reading: Teacher's, Curriculum, Control
- Essay reading: Where are We Going?

Certificates are awarded through a Christian school affiliated with any of the above associations. For further information, contact Nehemiah Institute at:

Nehemiah Institute
554 Groves End Lane
Winter Garden, FL 34787
1-800-948-3101
office@nehemiahinstitute.com

Recommended Reading

The resources are recommended for all Christians in that we all need to increase our understanding of the biblical worldview. They are especially recommended for Christian educators. "Christian educators" includes pastors, principals, administrators, teachers, school board members, and home schooling parents. Some of these resources are useful with students. In these cases it is noted in the commentaries.

Many of these books can be ordered through secular and Christian bookstores and Internet booksellers. Others may only be available through the ministries that published them. A list of websites of Christian ministries is included in this resource list.

A few of the authors on this list do not write from a Christian perspective. Others may be Christian but from a denomination or tradition that is different from your own. Their work is included in this list because they have certain insights that can be helpful in developing a biblical worldview. Secular authors are identified as such in the commentaries.

*--highly recommended
#--for use with children or youth (textbook)

Balmuth, Miriam. *The Roots of Phonics*. Baltimore: York Press, 1982.
Scholarly treatment of the nature of phonics.

Barton, David. "America's Godly Heritage" (video). Aledo, TX: WallBuilders, 1990. **Every Christian should see this video to be inspired as well as to be informed.**

* Barton, David. "Education and the Founding Fathers" (video). Aledo, TX: WallBuilders, 1993. **Great video for understanding the biblical foundations of American education. ***

* # Beliles, Mark A., and Stephen K McDowell. *America's Providential History*. Charlottesville, VA: Providence Foundation, 1989.
This is a must read for all Christians. This book is an excellent history of the Christian foundations of America. It will definitely strengthen the reader's biblical worldview. It is also an excellent textbook for the upper grades and high school.

Beliles, Mark A., and Stephen K. McDowell. *Liberating the Nations*. Charlottesville, VA: Providence Foundation, 1995.

Blumenfeld, Samuel L. *Is Public Education Necessary?* Boise, ID: The Paradigm Company, 1981.

* Blumenfeld, Samuel L. *NEA: Trojan Horse in American Education*. Boise, ID: The Paradigm Company, 1984.
Excellent for understanding the history of American Education.

Blumenfeld, Samuel L. *NEA: The Whole Language/OBE Fraud*. Boise, ID: The Paradigm Company, 1995.

Breese, Dave. *Seven Men Who Rule the World from the Grave*. Chicago: Moody Press, 1990.

119

Christian perspective of the influence of humanist thinkers on modern culture. Highly recommended for understanding the biblical worldview.

Dang, Katherine. *Universal History, Volume I.* Cincinnati: C.J. Krehbiel Co., 2000. Scholarly treatment of the difference between the pagan and biblical worldviews.

DeMar, Gary. *God and Government (Three Volumes).* Atlanta: American Vision, 1997.
Great explanation of the biblical principles of government. We highly recommend these books for use at the upper grades and high school level.

DeMar, Gary. *America's Christian History: The Untold Story.* Atlanta: American Vision, 1993.

* # DeMar, Gary, with Fred Douglas Young and Gary L. Todd. *Reformation to Colonization.* Atlanta: American Vision, 1977.
History free of humanistic revision. Highly recommended as a textbook for upper grade and high school history.

* # DeMar, Gary, and Fred Douglas Young. *A New World in View.* Atlanta: American Vision, 1996.
More history free of humanistic revision. Highly recommended for upper grade and high school history.

DeMar, Gary. *Thinking Straight in a Crooked World.* Powder Springs, GA: American Vision, 2001.
Recommended for all Christians for forming and strengthening their biblical worldview.

Dobson, James, and Gary L. Bauer. *Children at Risk.* Dallas: Word Publishing, 1990.

Eakman, B.K. *Educating for the New World Order.* Portland: Halcyon House, 1991. This book reveals the philosophical roots of the current trends in American education.

Edelsky, Carole, and Bess Altwerger and Barbara Flores. *Whole Language: What's the Difference?* Portsmouth, NH: Heinemann, 1991.
Written in support of the whole language philosophy, this book gives insight into the philosophical basis of whole language.

Evans, Pearl. *Hidden Danger in the Classroom.* Petaluma, CA: Small Helm Press, 1990. This book explains the failure and danger of Carl Roger's humanistic psychology.

Flesch, Rudolf Flesch. *Why Johnny Can't Read.* New York: Harper & Row, 1955.
The original criticism of the anti-phonics movement.

Flesch, Rudolf Flesch. *Why Johnny Still Can't Read.* New York: Harper & Row, 1981.

Foster. Marshall, and Mary Elaine Swanson. *The American Covenant: The Untold Story.* Thousand Oaks, CA: The Mayflower Institute, 1992.

Gabler, Mel and Nora, with James C. Hefley. *What Are They Teaching Our Children?* Wheaton, IL: Victor Books, 1987.

Hall, Verna M. *The Christian History of the Constitution of the United States of America.* San Francisco: Foundation for American Christian Education, 1966.
This classic has provided the philosophical basis for the current revival of interest in biblical worldview education.

* Hart, Benjamin. *Faith and Freedom.* Dallas: Lewis & Stanley, 1988.
Recommended as one of the best books in print for understanding the Christian foundation of America.

Hefley, James C. *Textbooks on Trail.* Wheaton, IL: Victor Books, 1976.

Hitchcock, James. *What is Secular Humanism?* Harrison, NY: RC Books, 1982.
This little book, written by a Catholic, is an excellent summary of the essence of secular humanism.

Howard, Donald R. *Crisis in Education.* Green Forrest, AR: New Leaf Press, 1990.

Johnson, Paul. *Intellectuals.* New York: Harper and Rowe, 1988.
Good historical background on some of the most influential humanist thinkers.

* Kennedy, D. James and Jerry Newcombe. *What if Jesus Had Never Been Born?* Nashville: Thomas Nelson, 1994.
Highly recommended for gaining an appreciation and historical perspective for the positive impact of Christianity on the world.

Kilpatrick, William. *The Emperor's New Clothes.* Ridgefield, CT: McCaffrey Publishing: 1985.
This book describes how modern psychology is more of a religion than a science.

Kilpatrick, William. *Psychological Seduction: The Failure of Modern Psychology.* Ridgefield, CT: McCaffrey Publishing: 1983.

Kurtz, Paul (editor). *Humanist Manifestos I and II.* Buffalo: Prometheus Books, 1973. **Christian educators should read these short documents to appreciate the hostility of humanism toward Christianity.**

Kurtz, Paul (editor). *Humanist Manifesto 2000.* Buffalo: Prometheus Books, 2000.
This is an updated summary of humanist belief.

Nash, Ronald H. *Worldviews in Conflict.* Grand Rapids: Zondervan, 1992.

Nye, Robert D. *Three Psychologies: Perspectives from Freud, Skinner, and Rogers.* Pacific Grove, CA: Brooks/Cole Publishing, 1975.
This little book provides a concise summary of the major psychological theories of the twentieth century, albeit from a secular perspective.

* # Noebel, David A. *Understanding the Times.* Manitou Springs, CO: Summit Press, 1991. **This book is the most comprehensive treatment of biblical worldview in print and is a must read for every Christian. Recommended as textbook for high school.**

* Overman, Christian. *Assumptions That Affect Our Lives.* Louisiana, MO: Micah Publishing, 1996. **This book is highly recommended for its insight into the difference between biblical and humanistic education.**

* Postman, Neil. *Amusing Ourselves to Death.* New York: Penguin Books, 1985. **Written as a secular commentary on contemporary America, this book has excellent insight into the culture's influence on education. It is highly recommended for all Christian educators.**

Quist, Allen. *FedEd.* Glencoe, MN: NuCompass Publishing, 2002. This book gives insight into how Goals 2000 establishes a national anti-biblical curriculum.

Rose, James B. *A Guide to American Christian Education for the Home and School: The Principal Approach.* Palo Alto, CA: American Christian History Institute, 1987.

* Rushdoony, Rousas J. *The Messianic Character of American Education.* Vallecito, CA: Ross House Books, 1963. Read this book for deep insight into the humanist influence in American education.

Rushdoony, Rousas J. *The Philosophy of the Christian Curriculum.* Vallecito, CA: Ross House Books, 1985.

* Schaeffer, Francis A. *How Should We Then Live?* Wheaton, IL: Crossway Books, 1976. **This classic is a must read for every Christian educator. The book provides historical perspective of the great conflict between humanism and the biblical worldview.**

Slater, Rosalie J. *Teaching and Learning America's Christian History.* San Francisco: Foundation for American Christian Education, 1965. **This scholarly classis is one of the foundational books for principal approach education.**

Smith, Carl B. (moderator). *Whole Language: The Debate.* Bloomington, IN: EDINFO Press, 1994. This book will erase any doubt that humanistic philosophy is behind the anti-phonics movement.

* # Smith, Ruth J. *The Mighty Works of God: Self-Government, A Child's History of The United States of America.* South Bend, IN: Bradford Press, 2002. Providential history for younger children.

Sowell, Thomas. *Inside American Education.* New York: Free Press, 1993.

Sproul, R.C. *Lifeviews.* Grand Rapids: Revell, 1986.

Stormer, John A. *None Dare Call It Education.* Florissant, MO: Liberty Bell Press, 1998.

Christian educators need to understand the negative trend in American education described in this book.

Stout, Maureen. *The Feel-Good Curriculum.* Cambridge, MA: Perseus Books, 2000. Even though the author does not write from a biblical worldview, this book is still helpful in understanding the dumbing down of America, particularly as it is affected by the self-esteem movement.

Sykes, Charles J. *Dumbing Down Our Kids.* New York: St. Martin's Press, 1995.

Vitz, Paul C. *Psychology as Religion.* Grand Rapids: William B. Eerdmans, 1977.

Wilson, Dennis and Dawn. *Christian Parenting in the Information Age.* Sierra Vista, AZ: TriCord Publishing, 1996.
This book stresses the importance of parenting from the biblical worldview.

Wilson, Douglas. *Recovering the Lost Tools of Learning.* Wheaton, IL: Crossway Books, 1991.

Wilson, Douglas. *The Case for Classical Christian Education.* Wheaton, IL: Crossway Books, 2003.

Additional Resources

Although you may not agree with every point of emphasis of each of these ministries, and neither does Nehemiah Institute give blanket endorsement, we believe the ministries on this list are the leading ministries in the Church today when it comes to educating in the biblical worldview.

American Vision: http://www.americanvision.org/
American Vision is a Christian education ministry providing education materials and information to assist individuals, families and churches develop a practical and dynamic biblical worldview. Since the belief and actions of individuals will affect the future of a nation, as lives are changed, our society will change. Many books are available and the magazine, Biblical Worldview, has been published monthly for nearly twenty years.

Answers in Genesis: http://answersingenesis.org/
Answers in Genesis is upholding the accuracy and authority of the Bible from its very first verse. Led by internationally known speaker and author Ken Ham, AiG conducts large seminars on Genesis, produces a daily radio program "Answers," prints the full-color magazine "Creation," and will soon build a large creation museum near Cincinnati.

Chalcedon Foundation: http://chalcedon.edu/
This is a conservative Christian organization founded on the work of Dr. R.J. Rushdoony. We believe their publication, the Chalcedon Report, is one of the best Christian publications available today.

Coalition on Revival: http://www.reformation.net/
This site provides several papers on a wide variety of topics, calling the church back to full obedience to scripture for all of life. The papers are written by scholars from all walks of Christendom, who share the conviction that the Bible is inerrant and authoritative.

Foundation for American Christian Education (FACE): http://www.face.net/
A very valuable Christian education website. FACE developed the Principle Approach, America's historic method of reasoning with the Truths of God's Word, and promotes it through The Noah Plan. Based on results of our PEERS Testing program, students from Principle Approach schools are substantially better educated in understanding and applying biblical principles to life. We highly recommend this program.

Institute for Creation Research: http://www.icr.org/
Another very good ministry promoting a literal interpretation of scripture regarding creation. Many excellent resources for home and school use.

The National Right to Read Foundation: http://www.nrrf.org/
Your best resource on the issue of teaching reading. Learn the truth about Whole Language and get the latest research on the effectiveness of phonics.

Nehemiah Institute: www.nehemiahinstitute.com
The founders of the original worldview-testing tool, the PEERS test, this ministry is recognized as the leading authority in worldview testing. Nehemiah also provides seminars for Christian educators and many other resources including this course.

Worldview Alliance: www.worldviewalliance.com
This is another resource from the Nehemiah Institute. It contains hundreds of excellent teaching papers from a wide variety of Christian scholars on topics related to PEERS.

Providence Foundation: http://www.providencefoundation.com/
This ministry has produced several very good resources among which are *America's Providential History* by Mark Beliles and Stephen McDowell. We consider this book essential reading for every Christian educator.

Summit Ministries: http://www.summit.org/
This is a wonderful ministry providing Christian worldview training to youth in summer camps (2 weeks in length). Their flagship publication, Understanding the Times (UTT) is excellent. Many youth have been put "on the right track" through this ministry.

Made in the USA
Middletown, DE
02 November 2022

13972127R00080